Safeguarding Democracy

A Warning to America and the World

Chris Moses

ISBN: 9798344707884

Table of Contents

Table of Contents

Introduction

In recent years, America's democratic fabric has been tested in ways that would have seemed unthinkable just a few decades ago. The foundational principles of governance, such as the rule of law, the separation of powers, and the integrity of electoral systems, have come under increasing strain. What was once the gold standard of democracy—the American experiment—now faces an existential challenge. For many observers, the political turbulence unfolding in the U.S. signals not just a momentary setback but a deep and systemic issue threatening to unravel the country's democratic institutions.

At the center of this crisis lies a series of controversial political actions, legal rulings, and societal divisions that have reshaped the country's political landscape. The latest Supreme Court ruling has added a new layer of complexity to an already precarious situation. For some, it is seen as a reaffirmation of constitutional boundaries, while for others, it represents a dangerous erosion of the checks and balances that protect the American democracy.

This book is not just an examination of these critical moments; it is a call to action. *A democracy cannot survive on autopilot. It requires constant maintenance, vigilance, and, most importantly, the participation of informed citizens.* As the November election looms, this call becomes even more urgent. The decisions made in this election will reverberate far beyond America's borders, influencing the global perception of democracy for generations to come.

- **Overview: America's Democracy is Under Threat**

The American democratic system, long held as an exemplary model of governance, now teeters on the edge of an unprecedented crisis. A combination of political polarization, systemic inequality, and the erosion of democratic norms have brought the country to a crossroads. At this moment in history, the question is not just about who wins the next election, but whether the very framework that has supported the United States for over two centuries can survive the mounting pressures.

At the core of this crisis is the recent ruling from the Supreme Court, a body that has increasingly found itself at the center of national controversies. The ruling, seen by many as favoring a political figure known for his disregard of legal norms, has set a precedent that may ripple through future generations. The decision effectively signals that even the highest court in the land is not immune to the growing partisanship and political maneuvering that have infected other branches of government. For critics, this ruling marks a dangerous shift in American jurisprudence—one that could have far-reaching implications for how laws are interpreted and enforced.

The implications extend far beyond the courtroom. This ruling could weaken the very pillars that hold up democratic governance, such as judicial impartiality and the rule of law. The growing perception that legal decisions can be swayed by political considerations diminishes public trust in the system, creating a fertile ground for further erosion of democratic norms. When the legal system itself begins to falter, the ripple effects are felt in every aspect of governance, from voting rights to the legitimacy of elected officials.

- **Key Themes**

- **The Challenge of Maintaining Democracy**

The true test of a democracy is not its ability to win wars or overcome economic downturns but to endure internal challenges that threaten its very existence. The United States of America is currently facing such a challenge. The rise of populist movements, the undermining of electoral processes, and the increasing power of fringe political actors have made the once-stable American democracy appear fragile. At its core, democracy depends on the belief that all citizens, regardless of status or wealth, have an equal say in governance. But when powerful political actors question the legitimacy of elections or seek to manipulate the system for their benefit, this belief begins to crumble.

Maintaining democracy requires more than adherence to written laws; it demands an unwritten social contract that values the peaceful transfer of power, the rights of minorities, and the rule of law. As political figures challenge these democratic norms, society must choose whether it will defend these principles or allow them to be eroded in the name of political expediency. It is not only politicians who are responsible for safeguarding democracy; it is the responsibility of every citizen, every institution, and every organization.

- **The Implications of Recent Political and Legal Developments**

The recent Supreme Court ruling, while legally binding, represents something far greater than a mere court decision. It illustrates a broader trend where political and legal systems have begun to shift away from impartiality and fairness toward an alignment with political ideologies. This sets a troubling precedent. When courts, which should act as neutral arbiters, are perceived as being influenced by political motivations, the very essence of justice is called into question.

This development is not isolated to the United States. Around the world, leaders in Hungary, Brazil, and Turkey have similarly eroded judicial independence, using courts to legitimize controversial actions and consolidate power. The American experience thus serves as a cautionary tale for other democracies that face similar threats to their judicial systems.

Moreover, the implications are not confined to the present moment. A legal precedent that favors political figures who seek to bend democratic norms can be used by future leaders to justify actions that further degrade the rule of law. If citizens begin to lose faith in the impartiality of the courts, the very foundation of democracy—the trust in fair and equal application of the law—will be at risk.

- **A Call to Action to Protect Democratic Values**

In light of these developments, the time for complacency has long passed. Democracy, especially in its most fragile moments, needs active defenders. The events unfolding in the United States should serve as a wake-up call, not just for Americans but for all who cherish democratic values worldwide.

Apathy is democracy's worst enemy. When citizens disengage from the political process, they cede control to those who would seek to undermine the system for personal or political gain. Protecting democratic values requires a renewed commitment to civic engagement, voter participation, and, most importantly, a recognition of the stakes involved. The erosion of democracy does not happen overnight; it happens incrementally, through small compromises and overlooked transgressions.

But the preservation of democratic ideals is possible, even in the face of overwhelming challenges. It requires a collective effort, a shared commitment to the principles that have sustained democratic governance for centuries. As this book explores, the defense of democracy is not just the responsibility of the political elite or the judiciary—it is the responsibility of every citizen, every voter, and every participant in the democratic process.

In conclusion, America stands at a pivotal moment in history. The upcoming election, the recent legal decisions, and the broader political climate have placed the country at the crossroads of democracy and authoritarianism. The choice is clear: either fight to preserve democratic values or risk losing them forever. This book and the discussions it seeks to provoke are a call to action for all who believe in the power of democracy and the importance of safeguarding it for future generations. The time to act is now.

- **A Global Wake-Up Call**

It's early morning in Washington, D.C. The sun rises over the Capitol, its golden rays illuminating the majestic dome, a symbol of democracy that has stood the test of time. Yet, beneath this iconic structure, the foundations of American democracy are shaking. The city that once epitomized the resilience of the democratic experiment now finds itself at the epicenter of a global crisis—a crisis that transcends borders and challenges the very essence of governance worldwide.

Thousands of miles away, in a bustling market in Lagos, Nigeria, vendors prepare for another day. The chatter of haggling and the aroma of street food fill the air as life goes on, seemingly untouched by the political turmoil in distant lands. Yet, the ripples of democracy's struggle are felt here too. In this young democracy, the stakes are high. The lessons from America and other nations are both cautionary and instructive, offering a roadmap for navigating the complex terrain of governance in the 21st century.

In Hungary's Budapest, the Danube River flows quietly under the Chain Bridge, a serene contrast to the political turbulence brewing in the parliament buildings. Here, the erosion of democratic norms is not a distant fear but a present reality. Once a beacon of democratic transition in Eastern Europe, Hungary now teeters on the edge of authoritarianism, a stark reminder of how fragile democracy can be.

From the streets of Hong Kong, where pro-democracy activists wave flags and chant slogans under the watchful eyes of an increasingly oppressive regime, to the rural heartlands of Brazil, where the landless poor fight for basic rights, democracy is under siege. These struggles, though separated by geography and culture, are united by a common thread—the fight to preserve the principles of freedom, justice, and equality in a world where these values are increasingly threatened.

The world is at a crossroads. The principles that have guided democratic governance for centuries are being questioned, eroded, and, in some cases, outright dismantled. In a time when the pace of change is accelerating and the lines between truth and falsehood are blurred, the very concept of democracy is being tested in ways we have never seen before.

- **The American Lens, The Global View**

This book is a wake-up call. While it may begin with an exploration of the American experience, its scope is global. America, often seen as the cradle of modern democracy, has served as both an inspiration and a cautionary tale. The strengths and weaknesses of its democratic system offer valuable lessons to nations across the globe—lessons that are more urgent now than ever.

In recent years, the cracks in the American democratic system have become increasingly visible. From the rise of populist rhetoric to the undermining of electoral processes, the challenges facing the United States are emblematic of a broader global struggle. But this book is not just about America—it is about the universal principles of democracy and the dangers that threaten them everywhere.

In countries as diverse as India, Poland, and Venezuela, the Benin Republic, the story is strikingly similar. Political leaders, emboldened by power and unchecked by weakened institutions, are pushing the boundaries of what is acceptable in a democracy. They challenge the independence of the judiciary, curtail press freedoms, and manipulate electoral systems to maintain their grip on power. The result is a slow but steady erosion of the democratic fabric, often unnoticed until it is too late.

- **A Warning to the World**

As you turn these pages, you will travel through time and across continents, exploring the rise and fall of democratic institutions, the battles fought to protect them, and the ever-present dangers that loom over them. You will read about the struggles of ordinary citizens—from the activists in Hong Kong risking their lives for freedom, to the students in Chile protesting for a more just society, to the women in Saudi Arabia fighting for the right to drive and vote. These stories, though diverse in their specifics, share a common urgency: the need to safeguard democracy.

This book is not a mere academic exercise or a historical recount. It is a call to action. It is a reminder that democracy is not a given; it is a choice, a responsibility that must be renewed with each generation. Whether you are reading this in a high-rise apartment in Tokyo, a village in Kenya, or a small town in the American Midwest, the message is the same: democracy is under threat, and its preservation requires vigilance, courage, and a commitment to the principles that underpin it.

- **The Time is Now**

We live in a time of unprecedented change—politically, technologically, and socially. The challenges facing democracy are multifaceted, and the solutions are not simple. But one thing is clear: the fight for democracy is a global one, and it demands a global response. The time to act is now.

As we embark on this journey together, we will explore the critical issues facing democracies today. We will examine the forces that seek to undermine them and the strategies that can protect them. Most importantly, we will confront the reality that the future of democracy is not just the responsibility of governments or politicians—it is the responsibility of every one of us.

In the words of former U.S. President Abraham Lincoln, democracy is "government of the people, by the people, for the people." But it will only endure if the people—everywhere—stand up to defend it.

This is our wake-up call. Let us heed it before it's
too late.

Chapter 1: The Erosion of Democracy

- **Historical Context**

The American experiment in democracy began with the Founding Fathers' vision, deeply rooted in the ideals of freedom, justice, and the sovereignty of the people. Their vision, encapsulated in the Declaration of Independence and later in the U.S. Constitution, sought to establish a system that would protect individual liberties while preventing any one person or group from gaining unchecked power. The revolutionary notion that government derives its legitimacy from the consent of the governed stood in stark contrast to the monarchies of the time, where rulers held absolute authority.

However, the system was far from perfect. When drafting the Constitution, the Founding Fathers grappled with compromises that would leave lasting scars on the fabric of American democracy. The institution of slavery, for instance, was maintained, and Native Americans, women, and non-landowning men were largely excluded from the political process. Despite these limitations, the groundwork was laid for a democratic system that would evolve over time through amendments and social movements.

Key historical moments have shaped and reshaped the trajectory of American democracy. The Civil War (1861-1865) marked the most significant internal conflict in U.S. history, testing the durability of the union and the principles of liberty and equality. At its core, the war was a battle over the future of democracy: Can a society that values individual freedom and autonomy permit the existence of slavery within its borders? The Union's victory and the subsequent Reconstruction period (1865-1877) promised a new era of civil rights for formerly enslaved people, but the failure to fully integrate these rights, particularly with the rise of Jim Crow laws, would hinder democracy for decades.

The Civil Rights Movement of the 1950s and 1960s, led by figures like Martin Luther King Jr., was a critical response to the exclusionary practices that had persisted. This movement challenged systemic racism, demanding equal rights for African Americans, including the right to vote. The passage of the Civil Rights Act of 1964 and the Voting Rights Act of 1965 represented significant victories, but they were hard-won battles in a nation still grappling with inequality.

Similarly, the Women's Suffrage Movement, culminating in the passage of the 19th Amendment in 1920, extended the right to vote to women, representing another critical expansion of democracy. These movements illustrate how democracy in America has been an ongoing project, constantly challenged and redefined by the people seeking to make the system live up to its ideals.

- **Current Threats**

The threats to democracy today echo many of the struggles of the past, though they have taken on new, often more sophisticated forms. One of the most prominent threats is voter suppression. While past tactics, such as literacy tests and poll taxes, were overtly designed to disenfranchise African Americans and other minority groups, modern-day voter suppression is subtler but no less damaging.

Today, tactics such as stringent voter ID laws, purging voter rolls, and reducing the number of polling places—particularly in minority and low-income areas—disproportionately impact marginalized communities. These efforts undermine the democratic process by making it more difficult for certain groups to participate, thus skewing representation and power in favor of those who already hold it.

The rise of disinformation is another significant threat. In an era where social media platforms have become the primary source of news for many, false information spreads rapidly, often unchecked. Disinformation campaigns, both foreign and domestic, exploit these platforms to sow confusion, distrust, and division. Whether it's a false claim about election fraud or misleading information about political candidates, the result is a populace that is unsure of what is true. This erosion of a shared understanding of reality is corrosive to democracy, which relies on an informed electorate making decisions based on facts.

Compounding these threats is the growing specter of authoritarianism. Across the globe, we've witnessed the rise of leaders who, while elected through democratic means, govern in increasingly autocratic ways. These leaders challenge democratic norms, weaken institutions, and consolidate power. In the U.S., these authoritarian tendencies are apparent in the undermining of the free press, the questioning of electoral outcomes, and the stacking of the judiciary with loyalists. Leaders who dismiss the rule of law and seek to stay in power by any means necessary pose an existential threat to democracy.

- **The Current State of Democracy**

The legitimacy of American democracy has been called into question more in recent years than at any point since the Civil War. The events surrounding recent elections, particularly the 2020 presidential election, have laid bare deep-seated issues within the electoral process and the broader political landscape. Allegations of widespread voter fraud, despite being thoroughly debunked, gained traction and were amplified by powerful figures and media outlets, leading to widespread distrust in the system.

This crisis of legitimacy culminated in the January 6th insurrection, when a violent mob stormed the U.S. Capitol trying to overturn the results of the election. The images of rioters breaking windows, attacking law enforcement, and occupying the halls of Congress shocked the world. More than just an attack on a building, this event was an attack on the democratic process itself. It was a chilling reminder that democracy, even in one of its oldest forms, is far from being invincible.

The January 6th insurrection also exposed how easily democratic norms can be eroded when leaders refuse to accept the results of elections. The peaceful transfer of power, a cornerstone of democracy, was thrown into jeopardy by a coordinated campaign to delegitimize the outcome. Even after the violence subsided, efforts to undermine voting rights continued. Legislators in various states introduced bills to limit access to the ballot, including restricting early voting, absentee voting, and imposing harsher voter ID laws.

These efforts, often justified under the guise of preventing voter fraud, disproportionately affect minority and low-income voters—the very communities that have historically faced the greatest barriers to democratic participation. The long-term implications of these legislative efforts are profound. By making it harder to vote, these laws not only disenfranchise millions of Americans but also weaken the overall legitimacy of the electoral process.

In addition, the rise of partisan gerrymandering continues to distort representation. Gerrymandering, the practice of drawing electoral districts to favor one party over another, undermines the principle of fair representation. By manipulating district boundaries, politicians can effectively choose their voters, rather than the other way around. This leads to a system where political power is concentrated in the hands of a few and the voices of ordinary citizens are diluted.

- **The Broader Implications**

The erosion of democracy in the U.S. has far-reaching implications, not just domestically but globally. As the world's oldest modern democracy, the United States has long been seen as a model for other nations. Its democratic institutions, while not perfect, have served as a blueprint for other countries striving to establish their own systems of governance. When democracy falters in the U.S., it sends a message to the world that democracy itself is vulnerable.

Authoritarian leaders around the globe take note when democratic norms are weakened in the U.S., using it as a justification for their own undemocratic actions. The erosion of American democracy emboldens these leaders, who point to the U.S. as proof that democracy is flawed and fragile. This creates a ripple effect, as the principles of democracy—free and fair elections, the rule of law, and the protection of civil liberties—are undermined worldwide.

At home, the continued erosion of democracy threatens the very fabric of American society. As trust in institutions declines, polarization increases. Political discourse becomes more toxic, and compromise becomes nearly impossible. In such an environment, governing becomes increasingly difficult, and the risk of further violence and instability grows.

The erosion of democracy in the United States is not an isolated event but part of a broader global trend. However, the stakes are particularly high in the U.S., where the long-standing traditions of democratic governance are being tested like never before. The historical context shows that democracy in America has always been a work in progress, constantly evolving through struggles and perseverance. But the current threats—voter suppression, disinformation, and authoritarianism—pose a unique danger to its future.

If these threats are not addressed, the very foundation of American democracy could crumble, with dire consequences for the nation and the world.

The fight to preserve democracy is not just the responsibility of elected officials; it is the responsibility of every citizen. Democracy, as history has shown, is both fragile and resilient. Whether it endures depends on the actions we take now to protect it.

Chapter 2: The Lawless Candidate

In the midst of a tumultuous political landscape, one figure stands as the embodiment of defiance against democratic norms—a candidate whose rise to power was marked by a disregard for the rule of law and ethical governance. We shall take a cursory gaze on the profile of this candidate, referred to here by a pseudonym to avoid direct confrontation, but whose behavior and impact on democracy are unmistakable. Through corruption, deceit, and a long record of undermining democratic institutions, this individual has not only challenged the pillars of democracy but also set a dangerous precedent for future leaders.

- **Profile of the Candidate**

The candidate we are examining represents a figure who has thrived on division, manipulation, and a flagrant disregard for the principles that uphold democratic governance. While this book opts for a pseudonym, the characteristics are clear—this person is a populist leader who thrives on charisma, incendiary rhetoric, and an ability to galvanize large sections of the electorate through fear and resentment. Unlike traditional political figures who build careers on public service, the lawless candidate has consistently sought to undermine public trust in institutions, presenting themselves as an outsider who is above the rules.

The candidate's history is mired in accusations of corruption, deceit, and self-interest. Even before entering the political arena, this individual was involved in a myriad of legal disputes, ranging from questionable business practices to allegations of fraud. Despite numerous investigations and indictments, the candidate has managed to evade accountability, leveraging legal technicalities, loyalists, and an unwavering base of supporters to sidestep consequences. This ability to evade justice is not merely a personal trait but has profound implications for the broader democratic system, as it signals to future leaders that the rule of law can be selectively applied.

- **The Candidate's History of Corruption and Deceit**

Corruption and deceit form the cornerstone of the candidate's political career. From the very beginning of their ascent, they have shown a willingness to flout the law and manipulate public opinion for personal and political gain. Key moments in their career highlight a pattern of behavior that involves obstruction of justice, abuse of power, and a deep-seated contempt for accountability.

One of the most significant examples of this pattern is the candidate's repeated attempts to obstruct justice. Throughout their time in office, numerous investigations have been launched to uncover the depths of their wrongdoings—whether it's interference in democratic processes, misuse of executive powers, or unethical dealings with foreign entities. These investigations have often been stymied by the candidate's use of their position to obstruct, intimidate, or fire investigators, creating a chilling effect on efforts to hold them accountable.

Abuse of power is another defining characteristic of this individual's record. Whether it's using the office to settle personal scores, pressuring government agencies to serve their interests, or manipulating law enforcement to protect their allies, the candidate has consistently treated public office as a means of personal enrichment and control rather than public service. Their tenure has been marked by scandals that would have ended the careers of most politicians, yet they have remained relatively unscathed due to a combination of media manipulation and unwavering loyalty from certain sectors of the electorate.

Perhaps most damaging, however, is the candidate's weaponization of misinformation. In a time when truth is already difficult to discern, the candidate has excelled in spreading falsehoods, conspiracy theories, and misleading claims. Whether it's questioning the legitimacy of elections, downplaying the severity of national crises, or demonizing opponents with baseless accusations, the candidate's mastery of disinformation has fundamentally undermined the democratic process. By creating a parallel reality in which facts are optional and loyalty to the candidate supersedes loyalty to the country, they have contributed to the degradation of public trust in institutions, the media, and the political process itself.

- **Implications of Electing a Lawless President**

The election of a lawless president carries significant and far-reaching implications, not just for the present moment but for the future of democracy itself. One of the most immediate consequences is the erosion of the rule of law. In a functioning democracy, laws are the bedrock upon which society is built, applying equally to all citizens, regardless of status. However, when the leader of a nation consistently evades accountability, it sends a dangerous signal that those in power are above the law. This undermines the very foundation of justice and weakens public confidence in the fairness of the legal system.

A lawless president also poses a direct threat to national security. History has shown that leaders who prioritize personal power over the national interest often engage in reckless and dangerous behavior on the global stage. Whether it's compromising national security by cozying up to authoritarian regimes, mismanaging crises, or engaging in corrupt dealings with foreign powers, the risks of electing such a figure are profound. The candidate's disregard for established norms and protocols means that sensitive information can be weaponized, alliances can be jeopardized, and adversaries can be emboldened. The stability of the global order, already fragile, is further threatened by the unpredictable and self-serving actions of a lawless president.

Beyond the structural implications, the election of such a candidate has devastating effects on the most vulnerable populations. A leader who governs without regard for laws, ethics, or decency is more likely to target marginalized communities, either through direct policy decisions or by emboldening violent extremists. Immigrants, people of color, the LGBTQ+ community, and others who rely on democratic protections are at heightened risk under such leadership. When laws are selectively enforced, or when leaders encourage discrimination and division, these groups often bear the brunt of systemic injustices.

- **The Candidate's Enablers**

No lawless leader operates in a vacuum. The candidate's rise to power and continued influence would not be possible without a network of enablers, including party loyalists, media outlets, and special interest groups. These enablers, often driven by short-term political or financial gain, play a crucial role in normalizing the candidate's behavior and shielding them from accountability.

Party loyalists are among the most visible enablers. Despite mounting evidence of corruption, abuse of power, and misconduct, members of the candidate's political party have consistently rallied around them, prioritizing party unity over the defense of democratic principles. These loyalists often dismiss criticism as partisan attacks, deflecting blame and creating an environment in which corruption is tolerated as long as it serves their interests. By refusing to hold the candidate accountable, they contribute to the erosion of democratic norms and set a precedent that future leaders can exploit.

Media outlets, particularly those that align ideologically with the candidate, also play a pivotal role in enabling their behavior. Through selective coverage, echoing misinformation, and providing a platform for conspiracy theories, these outlets help shape public opinion in favor of the candidate. By presenting a skewed version of reality, they create an alternative narrative that allows the candidate's supporters to dismiss legitimate criticism as fake news or politically motivated attacks.

Special interest groups, including wealthy donors and corporate allies, further enable the candidate by funding their campaigns and shielding them from financial scrutiny. These groups often benefit from the candidate's policies and are willing to overlook or excuse their lawlessness in exchange for favorable legislation. This relationship between money and politics amplifies the candidate's power, as they can rely on the financial backing of these groups to sustain their political career, regardless of public opinion.

- **Consequences of Normalization**

Perhaps the most dangerous consequence of electing a lawless candidate is the normalization of corruption and deceit. When misconduct becomes routine and unpunished, it ceases to be shocking. Gradually, society becomes desensitized to behavior that would have once been considered unacceptable. This normalization is particularly insidious because it lowers the bar for future leaders, making it easier for them to engage in similar or worse conduct without facing consequences.

The normalization of lawlessness also undermines public trust in government. When citizens see that their leaders can break laws with impunity, they begin to question whether the system is rigged in favor of the powerful. This cynicism erodes civic engagement as people become disillusioned with the idea that their participation in the democratic process can effect change. When trust in government is shattered, it creates fertile ground for extremism as people look for alternative solutions outside of the democratic system.

Furthermore, the acceptance of corruption and deceit as normal has long-term consequences for the country's international standing. The U.S., once seen as a global leader in promoting democracy and the rule of law, loses credibility when it elects leaders who embody the opposite values. This decline in moral authority weakens the U.S.'s ability to advocate for human rights, democratic reforms, and good governance around the world, further eroding the global democratic order.

The rise and election of a lawless candidate represent a fundamental challenge to democracy. This individual's history of corruption, deceit, and disregard for the rule of law is not just a personal failing but a threat to the very principles that sustain democratic governance. The enablers who surround them—party loyalists, media outlets, and special interest groups—only exacerbate the problem, allowing corruption to become normalized.

The implications of electing such a candidate are profound. From the erosion of the rule of law to the weakening of national security and the endangerment of vulnerable populations, the consequences are far-reaching and deeply troubling. Ultimately, if corruption and lawlessness are allowed to thrive, democracy itself is at risk of being fundamentally altered, perhaps beyond repair. The fight to prevent this must be fought not just by political leaders but by citizens who refuse to accept deceit and corruption as the new normal.

Chapter 3: The Supreme Court's Failure

The Supreme Court, often regarded as the ultimate safeguard of the Constitution and protector of civil liberties, is expected to stand as an impartial arbiter in the face of political turbulence. However, recent decisions have revealed a troubling shift in the Court's role, suggesting that its function as a neutral check on executive and legislative power may be eroding. At this juncture, we explore a recent ruling that serves as a stark warning of the Court's failure to uphold its duties. Through an analysis of the legal context, majority, and dissenting opinions, we will also examine the grave consequences of this ruling and critique the Court's deviation from its foundational responsibilities.

- **Analysis of the Ruling**

The ruling in question is pivotal because it illustrates a profound shift in how the judiciary is interpreting its constitutional obligations. To fully grasp the significance of the decision, it's important to first understand the legal context in which it occurred. Historically, the Supreme Court has been the final word on interpreting the Constitution, ensuring that laws and executive actions do not infringe on individual rights or the balance of power outlined by the Founding Fathers. Key decisions like "Brown v. Board of Education" and "Roe v. Wade" showcased the Court's capacity to transcend politics in upholding the ideals of justice and equality.

However, in this recent ruling, the majority opinion took a decidedly different turn. In a case that called into question a fundamental right or principle—such as voting rights, reproductive autonomy, or executive overreach—the Court sided with those seeking to limit individual freedoms or grant greater power to the executive. This ruling didn't just reinterpret existing laws; it set a dangerous precedent by undermining long-established protections that had been considered the bedrock of American democracy. By ruling in favor of those who seek to restrict rights, the Court sent a clear message that certain freedoms, once assumed secure, are now open to reinterpretation or erosion.

The majority opinion, written by justices who have been criticized for their ideological biases, justified the ruling through a narrow, literal interpretation of the Constitution or by leaning on technicalities. This legalistic approach, while valid in certain instances, ignored the broader implications of the decision. It treated the case as an isolated issue rather than part of a larger, concerning trend in which civil liberties and democratic principles are being steadily chipped away.

In contrast, the dissenting opinion, authored by justices who recognized the dangers posed by this decision, warned of the far-reaching consequences. The dissent highlighted that this ruling not only stripped away essential rights but also emboldened those who seek to further consolidate power at the expense of the rule of law. The dissenting justices argued that the Court's duty is not merely to interpret the law in a vacuum but to consider the societal and constitutional consequences of its rulings. They emphasized the historical role of the Court in protecting the marginalized, warning that this ruling marks a dangerous departure from that tradition.

The consequences of this ruling are both immediate and long-term, and they strike at the very heart of the democratic system. At its core, this decision represents a clear erosion of the rule of law—the very principle that all individuals, regardless of their position, are subject to the same legal standards. When the highest court in the land signals that certain rights are negotiable or that certain individuals are above scrutiny, it sets a dangerous precedent for the future.

One of the most alarming consequences is the empowerment of authoritarianism. Historically, authoritarian regimes have risen when institutions designed to check executive power are weakened or co-opted. When the judiciary, the last bastion of impartiality, begins to favor those in power rather than holding them accountable, it paves the way for the erosion of democratic norms. Leaders who previously might have hesitated to push the boundaries of their authority now feel emboldened, knowing that the courts will not stand in their way. This ruling not only grants unchecked power to the executive branch but also sends a message to future leaders that they, too, can operate with impunity if they control or manipulate the judiciary.

Beyond the immediate political implications, this ruling also signals to the public that certain fundamental rights are no longer guaranteed. In a democracy, the assurance that individual liberties are protected by the Constitution fosters public trust in institutions. However, when the Supreme Court begins to selectively reinterpret those protections, it creates uncertainty and disillusionment among citizens. This disillusionment can lead to decreased civic participation, as people feel their voices and votes no longer matter in a system that seems rigged in favor of the powerful. Over time, this erodes the very fabric of democracy, leading to a more passive or disengaged electorate.

Additionally, the ruling has global consequences. For much of the modern era, the U.S. has been viewed as a beacon of democracy and human rights. Other nations, especially those in nascent or fragile democracies, have looked to the U.S. Supreme Court as a model for impartiality and justice. However, this decision undermines that global perception, sending a signal that the rule of law is not as sacrosanct as once believed. Authoritarian leaders abroad may feel validated by this ruling, using it to justify their own attacks on judicial independence and individual rights. The ripple effect could embolden anti-democratic movements worldwide.

- **Critique of the Court's Role**

The failure of the Supreme Court in this ruling is not merely a matter of disagreement over legal interpretation; it represents a fundamental abandonment of its duty to act as a check on power. The Court's role in the American system of governance is to act as a guardian of the Constitution, ensuring that no branch of government oversteps its bounds and that the rights of individuals are protected. By siding with those who seek to erode these rights, the Court has abdicated this responsibility.

One of the most troubling aspects of this ruling is that it reflects a shift in the Court's priorities. Rather than standing above the political fray, the Court has become increasingly politicized, with decisions that seem to reflect the ideological leanings of the justices rather than a faithful interpretation of the law. While the judiciary has always been influenced by politics to some degree, recent appointments have shifted the balance so far that many Americans now view the Court as an extension of the executive or legislative branches rather than an independent body. This perception of bias further undermines public trust in the institution.

Moreover, by ruling in favor of those who seek to undermine democratic norms, the Court has failed in its most basic function: to act as a check on power. The Founding Fathers designed the American system of government with the understanding that unchecked power leads to tyranny. The Supreme Court was intended to be the ultimate safeguard against such abuses. Yet in this ruling, the Court not only failed to check power but actively enabled its expansion. This is particularly alarming in a time when authoritarian tendencies are on the rise, both in the U.S. and globally. When the judiciary abdicates its responsibility to hold leaders accountable, it leaves the door wide open for further abuses of power.

The Court's failure in this instance is also a failure of imagination. Rather than recognizing the broader societal implications of its ruling, the majority opinion relied on narrow legal interpretations that ignored the real-world consequences. This kind of judicial myopia is dangerous because it divorces the law from the lived experiences of the people it is supposed to serve. A court that rules in favor of those in power while ignoring the impact on the marginalized is not a court that is fulfilling its constitutional duty.

The Supreme Court's recent ruling represents a significant failure in its role as a protector of democracy and the rule of law. By siding with those who seek to erode rights and empower authoritarianism, the Court has not only failed to check the abuse of power but has actively contributed to it. The consequences of this ruling are profound, both for the U.S. and for the global perception of democracy.

The Court's abandonment of its duty as a check on power is particularly alarming in a time when democratic institutions are under siege. This ruling, and others like it, signal a troubling shift in the Court's priorities, one that places ideology above impartiality and political expedience above the protection of individual rights. If the Supreme Court continues down this path, it risks not only its own legitimacy but the very survival of American democracy.

This failure must serve as a wake-up call. The American people, as well as their elected representatives, must recognize the dangers posed by a judiciary that no longer functions as an independent check on power. Efforts to reform the Court, strengthen judicial independence, and restore public trust in the institution must be prioritized if democracy is to survive this critical moment.

Chapter 4: The Bedrock of Democracy

Democracy, as envisioned by its architects, is built upon a foundation of accountability. Without mechanisms to hold individuals, institutions, and the government accountable for their actions, democracy quickly erodes into chaos or authoritarianism. Let's explore the critical role of accountability, emphasizing the systems of checks and balances, the rule of law, and the far-reaching consequences that arise when these foundational pillars are allowed to weaken. The rise of authoritarianism and the loss of trust in institutions are the inevitable outcomes of eroded accountability, leaving a fragile shell of what was once a functioning democracy.

- **The Importance of Accountability**

Accountability is the lifeblood of any healthy democracy. It is how power is kept in check, ensuring that no individual or group can amass unchecked authority. The Founding Fathers, in their design of the American government, embedded accountability into the structure of governance through two main principles: checks and balances and the rule of law. These principles serve as safeguards, intended to prevent any one branch of government or individual from overstepping their bounds and to ensure that citizens can trust their leaders to act in the public interest.

- **The Role of Checks and Balances**

Checks and balances are at the core of the U.S. system of governance, ensuring that power is distributed across the executive, legislative, and judicial branches. Each branch has the authority to limit the actions of the others, preventing any one branch from gaining too much control. This division of power is intended to foster collaboration, negotiation, and compromise, thus preventing tyranny by any one faction.

Historically, the checks and balances system has played a critical role in maintaining the integrity of American democracy. The judicial branch, for example, has struck down executive orders that exceeded presidential authority. The legislative branch has passed laws to correct executive overreach or judicial misinterpretation. The executive branch, in turn, has vetoed bills or used executive orders to check Congress's legislative powers when necessary. This interplay creates a dynamic where no single branch can dominate.

However, the effectiveness of this system relies on the willingness of each branch to fulfill its role without capitulating to the influence of the other branches. For example, if the legislature fails to act as a check on the executive by refusing to investigate misconduct or override vetoes when appropriate, the balance of power shifts. Similarly, when the judiciary allows itself to become politicized, it ceases to function as an impartial check on the executive or legislative branches.

In recent years, the system of checks and balances has been tested in unprecedented ways. There have been several instances where the executive branch has openly defied congressional subpoenas, refused to comply with oversight investigations, and used its authority to influence judicial appointments and rulings. The legislature, in many cases, has been either unwilling or unable to effectively check these overreaches due to partisan divisions. This weakening of checks and balances creates an environment where power becomes concentrated in the hands of a few, undermining the democratic principle that no one is above the law.

- **The Rule of Law**

If checks and balances are the framework of accountability, the rule of law is its foundation. The rule of law dictates that laws apply equally to everyone, regardless of position or power, and those laws must be fairly enforced. In a democracy, the rule of law ensures that government actions are transparent, predictable, and subject to oversight. It is what distinguishes democracies from autocracies, where laws are either arbitrarily enforced or designed to protect those in power at the expense of the public.

Our Founding Fathers envisioned a nation governed not by individuals but by laws. They recognized that power corrupts and that without clear, enforceable rules, leaders might exploit their positions for personal gain. The rule of law is the principle that ensures accountability by holding all individuals, from the president to the ordinary citizen, to the same legal standards.

However, the rule of law is vulnerable to erosion when it is selectively enforced or disregarded altogether. When leaders act with impunity, when the judiciary is used to shield the powerful from scrutiny, and when laws are applied unequally, the rule of law begins to break down. This erosion can be seen in cases where the legal system is manipulated to serve political purposes—such as in politically motivated investigations, the misuse of executive powers, or the shielding of corrupt officials from prosecution.

When citizens observe that the rule of law is not being upheld, it sends a message that certain people or groups are above the law. This not only undermines trust in the legal system but also diminishes the public's willingness to engage in democratic processes. After all, why participate in a system that seems rigged to protect the powerful? The erosion of the rule of law leads directly to cynicism and disengagement, further weakening democratic institutions.

When accountability fails—whether through the breakdown of checks and balances or the erosion of the rule of law—the consequences are severe and far-reaching. Perhaps the most alarming consequence is the rise of authoritarianism. As power becomes more concentrated and less subject to oversight, the conditions are ripe for authoritarian leaders to emerge. Simultaneously, the public's trust in institutions, which is vital for the functioning of democracy, begins to falter, leading to apathy, disengagement, and division.

- **The Rise of Authoritarianism**

Authoritarianism is the complete opposite of democracy. It is a system where power is concentrated in the hands of a single leader or a small group, with little to no accountability to the public or other branches of government. Once checks and balances have weakened and the rule of law is no longer enforced, the door opens for leaders to act with impunity. Without accountability, these leaders can manipulate the system to entrench their power—whether by stifling dissent, limiting free speech, manipulating elections, or disregarding the legal constraints that would otherwise hold them in check.

The rise of authoritarianism is often gradual. It begins with small erosions of accountability—perhaps the dismissal of key watchdog officials, the politicization of the judiciary, or the use of executive orders to bypass the legislative process. These actions might initially be justified as necessary for efficiency or security, but they set dangerous precedents. Over time, leaders who feel they are above the law become emboldened, pushing the boundaries of their power further and further. Before long, the system of governance begins to resemble less of a democracy and more of an autocracy, where the will of the people is secondary to the will of the leader.

In recent years, we have witnessed alarming trends in which some leaders seek to consolidate power through undermining democratic norms. This includes efforts to discredit the press, interfere with judicial processes, and delegitimize elections. These actions are textbook examples of authoritarianism taking root in a system where accountability has eroded. As these trends continue, they threaten to transform the nature of governance, turning what should be a government of the people into a government that exists solely to maintain the power of the few.

- **The Loss of Trust in Institutions**

Just as dangerous as the rise of authoritarianism is the accompanying loss of trust in democratic institutions. Institutions like the judiciary, legislature, and media are crucial for the proper functioning of democracy. When citizens lose faith in these institutions, democracy becomes vulnerable to collapse from within.

The loss of trust in institutions is often fueled by visible failures of accountability. When elected officials act without consequence, when judges make decisions that seem politically motivated, or when the media is seen as biased or controlled by special interests, public confidence in these institutions begins to erode. Citizens may come to believe that the system is rigged, that their voices don't matter, and that the institutions designed to protect their rights are instead protecting the powerful.

This loss of trust can manifest in various ways— lower voter turnout, increased political polarization, or the rise of populist movements that promise to "drain the swamp" or dismantle the system altogether. While these movements may emerge from a legitimate frustration with institutional failures, they can also be co-opted by authoritarian leaders who use public distrust as a tool to further undermine democratic processes.

Moreover, once trust in institutions has been lost, it is incredibly difficult to rebuild. Restoring faith in the system requires not only structural reforms but also a cultural shift toward transparency, fairness, and accountability. In the absence of such reforms, the loss of trust becomes a self-fulfilling prophecy: the more people lose faith in institutions, the less they participate, and the more corrupt or ineffective those institutions become.

Accountability is not merely a principle of good governance; it is the bedrock of democracy itself. Without checks and balances to limit the concentration of power and the rule of law to ensure equality before the law, democracy becomes hollow, leaving it vulnerable to authoritarianism and disillusionment. In today's political climate, the erosion of accountability is not an abstract concern—it is a clear and present danger.

The rise of authoritarianism and the loss of trust in institutions are the inevitable consequences of allowing accountability to falter. To protect democracy, we must strengthen the mechanisms that hold power in check and ensure that all leaders, regardless of their status, are subject to the same legal standards as ordinary citizens.

Only by reinforcing the principles of accountability can we ensure that democracy not only survives but thrives in the face of current challenges.

The survival of democratic governance depends on the restoration and strengthening of these fundamental principles. The people, through active engagement, must demand accountability from their leaders, rebuild trust in institutions, and work tirelessly to ensure that power remains in the hands of the people—not concentrated in the hands of the few.

Chapter 5: A Call to Action

In the grand narrative of democracy, the responsibility for its survival has always rested not only with leaders and institutions but with the people. At this critical moment, the fragility of democratic systems around the world has never been more apparent. We are living in an era of unprecedented challenges where the foundations of democracy are under siege. Yet, within this chaos lies an opportunity: the opportunity for ordinary people to rise, to reclaim their power, and to defend the democratic ideals that form the bedrock of free societies.

This is a rallying cry, a call to action for every citizen who values democracy and the freedoms it guarantees. The defense of democracy is not a passive act; it requires vigilance, courage, and most importantly, action. It demands that we see ourselves not just as beneficiaries of democracy but as its guardians.

- **Urgent Appeal: The Necessity of Defending Democracy**

Democracy, despite its noble ideals, is not self-sustaining. It requires constant care, active participation, and an unwavering commitment to its preservation. The notion that democracy will always prevail simply because it exists is one of the most dangerous assumptions we can make. History has repeatedly shown that even the most well-established democracies can fall prey to internal decay, external threats, or the slow erosion of the very principles that sustain them.

We are standing at a critical turning point today. Recent political and legal developments, both in the United States and around the world, have revealed how delicate democracy truly is. When voter suppression becomes normalized, when disinformation distorts public perception, and when elected officials flout the rule of law without consequence, democracy's future hangs in the balance.

The signs of democratic backsliding are everywhere, from the weakening of independent media to the politicization of the judiciary. For many, the temptation is to retreat, to disengage, to assume that the tide of authoritarianism will somehow recede on its own. But this is precisely the moment when action is most critical. Democracy cannot survive in a vacuum; it depends on the active involvement of its citizens to remain strong. And when those citizens fail to act, the forces that seek to dismantle democracy gain ground.

The urgency of defending democracy cannot be overstated. The threats we face today—authoritarianism, disinformation, corruption, and the erosion of trust in institutions—are not theoretical. They are real, and they are already reshaping the political landscape. To remain silent, to stay on the sidelines, is to allow these threats to grow unchecked.

This is not just a battle for the present but for the future. The actions we take today will determine whether the next generation inherits a robust democracy or a hollowed-out shell of one. It is time to recognize that democracy is not a gift that can be taken for granted; it is a responsibility that must be actively defended, nurtured, and protected.

- **Suggestions for Activism: How to Defend Democracy**

While the challenges facing democracy are daunting, the path forward is clear. Every individual, regardless of their background, has a role to play in safeguarding the democratic process. The key is to move beyond passivity and into action. Below are practical and essential ways in which each of us can contribute to the defense of democracy.

1. **Educating Oneself**

The first and most crucial step in defending democracy is education. To protect something, one must first understand it. This means learning about the democratic process, the institutions that uphold it, and the forces that seek to undermine it. It means understanding not just how democracy functions but also the ways in which it can fail.

The importance of staying informed cannot be overstated. In an age where disinformation spreads rapidly through social media, critical thinking becomes a powerful tool. Learning to differentiate between credible sources and misinformation is vital. By educating ourselves, we become less susceptible to manipulation and better equipped to engage in meaningful dialogue about the issues facing our democracy.

But education is not just about consuming information—it's about fostering a deeper understanding of civic responsibility. This means learning about the history of democratic struggles, the sacrifices made by those who came before us, and the ways in which democracy has been both strengthened and weakened over time. An educated citizenry is the backbone of any healthy democracy, and it is through knowledge that we can most effectively defend it.

2. **Getting Involved**

While education is critical, it is only the first step. Defending democracy requires action, and one of the most powerful ways to act is by getting involved in local and national political processes. Democracy is participatory by nature, and its strength lies in the active engagement of its citizens.

One way to get involved is by supporting democratic institutions. This might mean volunteering for voter registration drives, participating in local government meetings, or joining advocacy groups that promote democratic values. It could also mean working with organizations that fight against voter suppression, disinformation, and corruption. These grassroots efforts are often where the most significant impact is made, as they directly involve communities in the democratic process.

Additionally, being involved means holding elected officials accountable. Democracy functions best when there is an active dialogue between the people and their representatives. This can take the form of writing to elected officials, participating in peaceful protests, or supporting candidates who demonstrate a commitment to democratic principles. Elected leaders should be reminded constantly that they are answerable to the people, not to special interests or authoritarian tendencies.

3. **Supporting Independent Media**

An independent and free press is a fundamental pillar of democracy. It acts as a watchdog, holding those in power accountable and ensuring that the public is informed. However, independent media is under threat from both political forces seeking to undermine its credibility and the financial pressures of an evolving digital landscape.

Supporting independent media is critical to ensuring that truth and transparency remain central to public discourse. This support can take many forms, from subscribing to reputable news outlets to sharing credible sources on social media. It also means calling out misinformation when you see it and engaging in conversations that promote fact-based discussions rather than conspiracy theories or partisan rhetoric.

Independent journalism serves as a check on power, exposing corruption, uncovering abuses of authority, and bringing critical issues to light. Without a robust media landscape, the public would be left in the dark, vulnerable to manipulation by those who seek to distort reality for personal or political gain. By supporting independent media, we are helping to preserve one of the essential pillars of democracy.

4. **Voting**

Voting is not only a right but also a responsibility. It is one of the most direct ways in which individuals can influence the course of their democracy. While it may seem like a small action, the collective power of millions of voters has the potential to shape policy, leadership, and the direction of the nation.

However, voting involves more than simply showing up on the day of election. It's about being an informed voter—knowing the candidates, understanding the issues, and being aware of the implications of each decision made at the ballot box. It's about recognizing that local elections are just as important as national ones and that every vote has the power to contribute to the larger democratic process.

In recent years, voter suppression efforts have sought to undermine this fundamental right. From restrictive voter ID laws to the purging of voter rolls, these efforts disproportionately affect marginalized communities and weaken the democratic process. Defending democracy means not only casting your vote but also advocating for policies that ensure fair and equal access to the ballot for all citizens.

5. **Building Community Resilience**

Democracy is not just a political system—it is a way of life that thrives on participation, dialogue, and mutual respect. Building strong, resilient communities is a powerful form of activism. This means fostering relationships, engaging in constructive dialogue, and working together to address the needs of the community.

Community resilience can be built through local organizations, civic groups, and neighborhood associations. These spaces allow for open discussions about the challenges facing democracy and provide a platform for collective action. By working together, communities can push back against efforts to divide them and ensure that democracy remains vibrant and responsive to the needs of all people.

- **The Power of Collective Action**

In the face of rising authoritarianism, disinformation, and political polarization, the defense of democracy may feel overwhelming. Yet history has shown that when people come together, they have the power to enact profound change. Collective action—whether in the form of education, civic engagement, media support, voting, or community-building—can fortify democracy against those who seek to undermine it.

Every citizen has a role to play, and the time for action is now. Democracy is not guaranteed; it is earned and maintained through vigilance and participation. As we confront the challenges of the present, let us remember that the future of democracy depends on the actions we take today. The power to protect democracy rests not in the hands of a few but in the collective will of the people. By answering this call to action, we not only defend the values that underpin democratic societies, but we also ensure that future generations will inherit a system of governance that truly represents the people.

The question before us is simple: Will we act, or will we allow democracy to slip through our fingers? The answer lies in the choices we make now, in the steps we take to stand up, speak out, and protect the freedoms we hold dear. Let this be a moment of awakening, a time when citizens rise together to ensure that democracy not only survives but thrives for generations to come.

Chapter 6: Words That Divide

- **The Power of Rhetoric**

In the quiet of a late evening, as the sun sets behind the horizon, there's a moment when the world seems to pause. It is in these moments that one can reflect on the power of words—how a single sentence can ripple through time, leaving indelible marks on history. Throughout the annals of time, words have shaped empires, toppled regimes, and ignited movements. They are the building blocks of human civilization, as vital as the bricks and mortar of ancient cities.

In an era where words have the power to cross borders within seconds, the impact of rhetoric has never been more significant. Words have always shaped societies, sparked revolutions, and built movements, but today they carry an added intensity. ***With every statement broadcasted to millions on social media or national television, rhetoric can unite or divide, inspire or inflame***. The power of language in the political arena is especially potent, often wielded as a tool to divide rather than to bring people together.

Divisive rhetoric, especially when coming from those in positions of influence, leaves lasting marks on societies. It stokes fear, hatred, and mistrust. We've seen it before in history—from the speeches of demagogues who manipulated words to serve their ambitions to the use of propaganda in regimes that sought to control entire populations. However, the modern age has amplified the reach of such rhetoric in ways previously unimaginable.

Consider the subtle shift in political language in recent years. Phrases that were once deemed extreme have become normalized. Divisive rhetoric is no longer an anomaly—it is a strategy. When a leader labels entire groups of people as criminals, invaders, or enemies of the state, it ignites the spark of "us vs. them," a dangerous that weakens the social fabric. Political rhetoric that reduces complex societal issues to soundbites thrives in a climate of oversimplification, where nuance is discarded for the sake of rallying a base.

The impact of divisive language extends beyond the political sphere. It creeps into everyday conversations, normalizing hostility and sowing seeds of division among neighbors, families, and communities. Words have the power to shift public perception, often creating echo chambers where individuals are only exposed to narratives that reinforce their pre-existing beliefs. In these spaces, critical thinking takes a back seat to emotional responses, making it easier for politicians and influential figures to manipulate public opinion.

- **Media and Public Discourse**

The media plays a central role in the amplification of rhetoric, both divisive and unifying. In a world where sensationalism often drives ratings, the media can become a megaphone for language that deepens societal divides. It's not just what is reported, but how it is reported. Soundbites, sensational headlines, and selective coverage fuel polarization. The more inflammatory a statement, the more likely it is to be replayed, dissected, and debated. The media, intentionally or not, becomes a key player in reinforcing these divisions.

Take, for instance, the way news outlets frame political controversies. Some platforms openly cater to specific ideological leanings, shaping narratives in ways that appeal to their core audience while alienating others. This selective reporting can skew public perception, making it harder for people to distinguish between facts and opinions. Instead of promoting informed dialogue, the media often perpetuates the cycle of divisive rhetoric, inadvertently becoming an agent in the erosion of civil discourse.

Social media platforms add another layer to this issue, with algorithms designed to show users content that aligns with their beliefs rather than challenging them. These platforms create echo chambers where people are bombarded with messages that reinforce their views, while dissenting opinions are filtered out. This echo chamber effect further polarizes societies, making constructive dialogue almost impossible.
When political leaders use rhetoric to inflame tensions and the media amplifies those messages, public discourse becomes toxic. This toxicity seeps into everyday conversations, deepening divisions and eroding trust in institutions. The idea of "agreeing to disagree" fades, replaced by an atmosphere where disagreement means outright hostility. The consequences of this shift are profound: it becomes harder to find common ground, and the idea of a shared national identity weakens.

- **Rebuilding Dialogue**

But it doesn't have to be this way. Words, when used thoughtfully, have the power to heal just as much as they can divide. The same platforms that amplify harmful rhetoric can also promote understanding, empathy, and respect for differences. This chapter, more than any other, calls upon leaders, citizens, and the media to take responsibility for the language they use and the conversations they foster. Constructive discourse, grounded in facts and empathy, can bridge divides and restore a sense of shared purpose in society.

The road to rebuilding dialogue starts with recognizing the power of words. It's about resisting the allure of inflammatory language, even when it seems expedient. It's about choosing rhetoric that unites rather than divides, that seeks common ground rather than exploiting differences. Leaders, the media, and citizens all have a role to play in this effort. It begins with accountability and the understanding that the words we use today will shape the world we live in tomorrow.

As individuals, we must also take responsibility for the words we consume and spread. It is easy to share a headline or retweet a post that stirs outrage, but more difficult to engage in thoughtful dialogue. However, if we are serious about protecting democracy, this is where the work begins. Democracy thrives on debate, but it must be the kind of debate that is grounded in respect, truth, and a commitment to the common good. Only then can we begin to mend the divisions that have torn at the fabric of society.

This serves as a wake-up call, not only for those in power but for each of us. It is a reminder that while words may seem fleeting, their impact is long-lasting. The rhetoric of today will shape the policies and ideologies of tomorrow. Let us be mindful of the words we choose and let them be words that build rather than divide. The future of our democracy relies on it.

Chapter 7: Misinformation and the Threat to Truth

In the digital age, where information is as abundant as the air we breathe, the truth is increasingly becoming a rare commodity. The unprecedented speed at which news and information travel has transformed our world into a global village, but it has also given rise to an insidious force: misinformation.

- **The Age of Disinformation**

Imagine a time when a rumor could only spread as far as the town square, limited by the reach of the human voice or the circulation of a printed pamphlet. Today, a single tweet can spark a wildfire of misinformation, crossing oceans and penetrating borders in a matter of seconds. The digital revolution, while empowering in many ways, has also provided fertile ground for the rapid dissemination of falsehoods, half-truths, and outright lies.

In the age of disinformation, the line between fact and fiction has become increasingly blurred. Social media platforms, with their vast reach and influence, have become the primary battlegrounds where truth is contested. Here, misinformation spreads like a virus, exploiting the very algorithms designed to keep us engaged. These platforms prioritize content that generates the most interaction, often favoring sensationalism over accuracy. As a result, the more outrageous or emotionally charged a piece of information is, the more likely it is to be shared, liked, and commented on, regardless of its veracity.

The impact of this disinformation on democratic processes is profound. Democracy relies on an informed citizenry—people who can make decisions based on accurate and reliable information. When misinformation takes root, it distorts public perception, creating a reality that is divorced from the truth. Elections serve as a key example of this phenomenon. False claims about voter fraud, rigged elections, or manipulated results can erode trust in the electoral process, leading to widespread disillusionment and disengagement.

Consider the aftermath of contentious elections in various parts of the world, where misinformation campaigns have sown doubt and division. In some cases, these campaigns have been orchestrated by foreign actors seeking to destabilize democracies, while in others, they have been the work of domestic groups aiming to suppress voter turnout or delegitimize the opposition. The result is the same: a fractured society, where citizens no longer trust the institutions that underpin their democracy.

The consequences of disinformation extend beyond the ballot box. Public health crises, such as the COVID-19 pandemic, have been exacerbated by the spread of false information. Misleading claims about the virus, its origins, and the effectiveness of vaccines have led to confusion, fear, and, in some cases, deadly outcomes. The pandemic has laid bare the dangers of living in a post-truth era where facts are seen as malleable and opinions are given the same weight as evidence-based science.

The age of disinformation is characterized by a paradox: never before have we had so much access to information, yet never before have we been so susceptible to being misled. The sheer volume of content available online makes it difficult to distinguish between credible sources and those peddling falsehoods. This information overload can lead to what experts call "information fatigue," where individuals become so overwhelmed that they are more likely to accept misinformation simply because it is easier than sifting through the noise to find the truth.

- **Critical Thinking: Tools for Discerning Fact from Fiction**

In this era of disinformation, the ability to think critically is more important than ever. Critical thinking is the antidote to misinformation, a skill that enables individuals to evaluate the credibility of sources, analyze the logic of arguments, and recognize cognitive biases that can cloud judgment. It is the foundation upon which informed citizenship rests.

But what does it mean to think critically? At its core, critical thinking involves a willingness to question assumptions, to seek out evidence, and to consider multiple perspectives before reaching a conclusion. It requires an understanding of the various techniques used to manipulate information, such as selective omission, false equivalence, and emotional appeals. In the age of disinformation, these skills are essential for anyone who wishes to navigate the complex and often deceptive landscape of modern media.

One of the first steps in developing critical thinking skills is to become aware of the biases that can influence our perception of information. Confirmation bias, for example, is the tendency to seek out and give more weight to information that confirms our existing beliefs while dismissing or ignoring evidence that contradicts them. This bias is particularly dangerous in the context of social media, where algorithms are designed to show us content that aligns with our preferences, creating echo chambers that reinforce our views and make us more susceptible to misinformation.

To counteract this bias, it is important to seek out diverse sources of information and to be open to perspectives that challenge our assumptions. This means actively engaging with news outlets and voices that represent different ideological viewpoints, rather than relying solely on sources that confirm what we already believe. It also means being willing to change our minds in the face of new evidence rather than clinging to beliefs that have been debunked or discredited.

Another key aspect of critical thinking is the ability to evaluate the credibility of sources. In the digital age, anyone can publish information online, making it difficult to distinguish between reputable sources and those that lack credibility. A critical thinker must be able to assess the reliability of a source by considering factors such as the author's credentials, the quality of the evidence presented, and the transparency of the source's funding and affiliations. This requires a healthy dose of skepticism, but not cynicism—a critical thinker does not reject information outright but rather evaluates it carefully before accepting it as true.

In addition to evaluating sources, critical thinkers must also be able to analyze the logic of arguments. Logical fallacies—errors in reasoning that undermine the validity of an argument—are common in misinformation. These include ad hominem attacks, where the focus is shifted from the argument to the person making it; straw man arguments, where an opponent's position is misrepresented to make it easier to attack; and false dilemmas, where a complex issue is presented as a choice between two extremes. Recognizing these fallacies is crucial for discerning fact from fiction, as they are often used to manipulate public opinion.

Critical thinking also involves recognizing the role of emotions in shaping our responses to information. Misinformation often relies on emotional appeals, such as fear, anger, or outrage, to override rational analysis. A critical thinker must be able to separate emotional reactions from logical reasoning, asking whether the information presented is supported by evidence rather than simply responding to how it makes them feel.

One of the most effective tools for promoting critical thinking is media literacy education. Media literacy teaches individuals how to critically analyze media messages, understand the techniques used to influence audiences, and recognize the role of the media in shaping public perception. In an age where misinformation is pervasive, media literacy is an essential skill for all citizens, empowering them to navigate the complex information landscape and make informed decisions.

However, critical thinking is not just an individual skill; it is also a collective responsibility. In a democracy, the health of public discourse depends on the ability of citizens to engage in reasoned debate, to challenge misinformation, and to hold those in power accountable. This requires a culture that values truth and transparency, where the pursuit of knowledge is seen as a shared endeavor rather than a competition to see who can shout the loudest.

- **The Path Forward: Reclaiming Truth in a Post-Truth Era**

The rise of misinformation presents a formidable challenge to democracy, but it is not an insurmountable one. By fostering critical thinking skills and promoting media literacy, we can equip individuals with the tools they need to navigate the age of disinformation. However, this is only part of the solution. Reclaiming truth in a post-truth era also requires systemic changes, including greater accountability for those who spread misinformation and more robust regulations for social media platforms.

One possible approach is to strengthen the oversight of online platforms, holding them accountable for the content they host and the algorithms they use to promote it. This could involve requiring platforms to take more proactive measures to identify and remove false information, as well as to provide users with greater transparency about how their data is used and how content is curated. Additionally, there could be stronger penalties for those who deliberately spread misinformation, particularly when it has the potential to cause harm.

Another important step is to support independent journalism and fact-checking organizations, which play a crucial role in countering misinformation. In an era where trust in the media is at an all-time low, it is essential to rebuild public confidence in credible sources of information. This means investing in quality journalism that adheres to rigorous ethical standards, as well as promoting fact-checking initiatives that can quickly debunk false claims and provide the public with accurate information.

Education also has a vital role to play in the fight against misinformation. By integrating critical thinking and media literacy into the curriculum from an early age, we can prepare future generations to be discerning consumers of information. This education should not be limited to schools but should also be extended to adults through public awareness campaigns and community programs.

Ultimately, the fight against misinformation is a fight for the very soul of democracy. In a world where falsehoods can spread faster than the truth, it is more important than ever to uphold the principles of transparency, accountability, and informed citizenship. By cultivating a culture of critical thinking and media literacy, we can ensure that democracy does not fall victim to the age of disinformation but rather emerges stronger and more resilient.

The path forward will not be easy, but it is one that we must take if we are to safeguard the integrity of our democratic institutions. The stakes are too high to ignore. In the words of Thomas Jefferson, "An informed citizenry is at the heart of a dynamic democracy."

Chapter 8: The Judiciary Under Siege

In the framework of a healthy democracy, the judiciary stands as a pillar of justice, balance, and impartiality. It is the silent guardian that ensures the law remains a tool for fairness, not a weapon of oppression. However, this crucial institution is under threat in ways that would have been unthinkable just a few decades ago. As political winds shift, so too do attempts to undermine the independence and integrity of the judiciary. Let's explore the critical role of an impartial judiciary in safeguarding democracy and examine the increasingly aggressive efforts to weaken its foundations.

- **Judicial Independence: The Cornerstone of Democracy**

The judiciary's role in a democracy is unique. Unlike the executive or legislative branches, which are designed to represent the will of the people or the interests of political parties, the judiciary is meant to remain above the fray. Its purpose is not to be swayed by the changing tides of popular opinion but to interpret and apply the law in a manner that is fair, unbiased, and consistent with the principles of justice.

Judicial independence ensures that judges can make decisions free from political pressure, personal bias, or external influence. It means that the courts must remain insulated from the influence of other branches of government and from the influence of those in power. Therefore, the concept of "separation of powers" is so fundamental to democracy. Each branch of government—the executive, the legislature, and the judiciary—has its own distinct role, and no branch should have control over the others.

Without an independent judiciary, the rule of law would crumble. The courts would no longer serve as impartial arbiters but could be co-opted to serve the interests of those in power. Imagine a world where political leaders could direct the judiciary to convict their opponents, exonerate their allies, or redefine the laws to suit their agendas. The very foundation of justice would become a tool for political manipulation, and the rights of individuals, especially the vulnerable, would be at the mercy of authoritarian whims.

Throughout history, the independence of the judiciary has been both celebrated and tested. The ideal of judicial independence stretches back centuries, rooted in the belief that justice must be blind to power, wealth, and influence. It was enshrined in democratic systems around the world to protect individuals from the excesses of tyranny. The courts became the last line of defense for civil liberties, human rights, and the protection of minorities against the will of the majority.

Yet, judicial independence is not guaranteed by mere tradition or idealism; it must be continually upheld by robust legal frameworks and public vigilance. Countries where this independence has been compromised have often seen a rapid decline in democratic norms. When courts are manipulated or corrupted, the legal system becomes little more than a facade of justice, a hollow shell where verdicts serve the interests of the ruling elite, not the people.

Judicial independence also plays a vital role in maintaining the checks and balances between branches of government. When courts hold the executive or legislature accountable, they prevent the accumulation of power in a single branch, which is the essence of authoritarianism. Through judicial review, courts can strike down unconstitutional laws, prevent abuses of power, and ensure that no one, not even the president or prime minister, is above the law.

In a truly independent judiciary, judges are selected based on their qualifications, experience, and commitment to the rule of law, not their political allegiances. Once appointed, they are shielded from undue influence by guarantees such as life tenure, appropriate compensation, and protection against arbitrary removal. These safeguards are not just bureaucratic details—they are the essential protections that allow judges to rule fairly, even in the face of pressure from powerful political actors.

- **The Assault on Democracy's Guardians**

Despite the clear importance of an independent judiciary, there have been increasing efforts worldwide to undermine the courts and bend them to political will. These threats come in many forms: direct attacks on individual judges, efforts to pack courts with loyalists, legislative moves to curtail judicial power, and a growing trend of delegitimizing courts in the eyes of the public.

One of the most direct threats to judicial integrity is the manipulation of judicial appointments. In recent years, political leaders in various democracies have sought to fill courts with judges who are seen as sympathetic to their agendas. By stacking the courts with ideologically aligned judges, politicians can ensure that judicial decisions align with their interests. The problem with this approach is not just that it politicizes the courts; it erodes public trust in the judiciary as an impartial institution. When citizens come to view the courts as extensions of political power, the very legitimacy of the judiciary is called into question.

Court-packing—the expansion of the number of judges in a court, often with the aim of altering its ideological balance—is another strategy employed to undermine judicial independence. This tactic allows those in power to dilute the influence of sitting judges by increasing the number of judges sympathetic to their policies. While court-packing is often framed as a necessary reform, it is a dangerous tool that can destabilize the judiciary and erode its credibility.

Another form of attack comes in the guise of legislative efforts to limit the scope of judicial review or weaken the courts' ability to check the power of the executive. Politicians, frustrated by unfavorable court rulings, may seek to pass laws that curtail the judiciary's power to review certain actions or that strip courts of their ability to rule on key issues. This is a subtle yet profound threat, as it limits the judiciary's capacity to serve as a counterbalance to unchecked power.

Moreover, personal attacks on judges have become more common, especially in politically charged cases. Judges who rule against powerful interests may find themselves subject to public vilification, harassment, or threats. Political leaders may use inflammatory rhetoric to discredit judges, accusing them of bias or corruption when they issue unfavorable rulings. These attacks not only endanger the physical safety of judges but also undermine the public's confidence in the judiciary as an institution of fairness and justice.

The weaponization of rhetoric against judges is particularly dangerous in democratic societies where the courts must remain an impartial and respected institution. When leaders frame the judiciary as an obstacle to their agenda rather than as an independent check on power, they erode the public's trust in the rule of law. This erosion of trust can lead to a dangerous situation where citizens begin to view court decisions as politically motivated rather than based on legal principles.

Consider the case of judicial reforms in countries where political leaders have sought to weaken the courts under the guise of "reform." These reforms often include measures to increase political control over judicial appointments, to limit the powers of judicial review, or to reorganize the judiciary in ways that diminish its independence. While such reforms are framed as necessary adjustments to an inefficient system, they often represent an assault on the judiciary's role as a protector of the Constitution and individual rights.

Additionally, the judiciary's independence can be threatened through budgetary manipulation. In some cases, governments have reduced funding for courts, limiting their ability to operate effectively and undermining their capacity to handle cases in a timely manner. By financially strangling the judiciary, governments can weaken its ability to serve as an effective check on power, further eroding public trust in the legal system.

Yet another subtle but pervasive threat is the gradual erosion of judicial norms and ethics. While many of these threats are explicit—such as political interference or court-packing—others are more insidious, taking the form of subtle pressures on judges to conform to prevailing political winds. For instance, in environments where the judiciary is increasingly politicized, judges may feel internal or external pressure to issue rulings that align with the interests of those in power rather than based solely on legal precedent and principles.

As we observe these trends across the globe, it becomes clear that the judiciary is not only under siege but is also becoming a battlefield where the future of democracy is contested. When the courts can no longer be relied upon to impartially interpret the law, democracy itself is in danger. Without an independent judiciary, the rights of individuals are no longer guaranteed, and the rule of law becomes a hollow concept.

- **Restoring and Defending Judicial Integrity**

The threats facing the judiciary today are serious, but they are not insurmountable. Restoring faith in the courts and defending judicial independence must be a priority for anyone committed to the preservation of democracy. This effort requires a multifaceted approach, involving legal, institutional, and societal changes.

First, the legal frameworks that protect judicial independence must be strengthened. Judicial appointments should be made based on merit, not political loyalty. To achieve this, transparent and depoliticized processes for selecting judges must be established, ensuring that only qualified and impartial candidates are appointed to the bench. This may involve creating independent judicial appointment commissions that operate free from political influence.

Second, the judiciary itself must take an active role in defending its independence. Judges must be willing to speak out when their autonomy is threatened, even if doing so puts them at odds with political leaders. Judicial associations and organizations can play a vital role in advocating for the protection of judicial independence and calling attention to attempts to undermine it.

Third, the public must be educated about the role and importance of an independent judiciary. When citizens understand that the courts serve as their last line of defense against tyranny and oppression, they are more likely to support measures that protect judicial independence. Public trust in the judiciary must be rebuilt through education campaigns that emphasize the importance of the rule of law and the impartiality of the courts.

Finally, efforts to undermine the judiciary must be met with robust legal and political opposition. Legislative efforts to weaken judicial review or limit the power of the courts should be challenged in the public sphere and, where possible, struck down by the courts themselves. Political leaders who attack the judiciary must be held accountable by their constituents and by the broader legal community.

The judiciary is the guardian of justice, the protector of individual rights, and the bulwark against authoritarianism. Its independence is not a luxury; it is a necessity for any functioning democracy. The integrity of the judiciary is what keeps the other branches of government in check and ensures that no individual, no matter how powerful, is above the law. Without it, the legal system is vulnerable to becoming a puppet of those in power, a mere tool to enforce their will.

- **The Global Assault on Judicial Independence: A Growing Trend**

In recent years, we have seen troubling trends across the globe where democratic backsliding has coincided with direct assaults on judicial independence. From Eastern Europe to Latin America, and even within some of the most established democracies, the judiciary has been increasingly targeted by regimes intent on consolidating power.

Poland offers a sobering example. Since 2015, the Polish government has enacted a series of judicial reforms that have weakened the independence of the courts. The ruling party passed laws allowing the government to control judicial appointments, giving political leaders the power to replace judges with those more favorable to their policies. These moves were met with widespread protests both domestically and internationally, but they highlight how easily a government can undermine judicial integrity under the guise of reform. The European Union even took unprecedented steps to intervene, recognizing the threat that a compromised judiciary posed to the rule of law across its member states.

Hungary provides a similar case study. Under Viktor Orbán's leadership, the judiciary has faced relentless pressure. Orbán's government implemented changes that allowed it to pack the Constitutional Court with loyalists while reducing the retirement age for judges, thus creating vacancies to be filled by government-approved candidates. This has effectively transformed Hungary's courts from independent arbiters into extensions of the executive branch, and the consequences have been far-reaching, from eroded civil liberties to the suppression of political dissent.

In Venezuela, the judiciary has been wholly captured by the executive branch, effectively dismantling any semblance of checks and balances. Courts have been used to disqualify political opponents, rubber stamp the actions of the ruling party, and undermine any attempt to challenge the authoritarian government. The courts, once a place of justice, have become instruments of oppression, a fate that serves as a grim reminder of the stakes involved when judicial independence is lost.

Even in the United States, where the judiciary has long been regarded as a beacon of independence, the courts have not been immune to politicization. The nomination and confirmation process for Supreme Court justices has become increasingly partisan, with judicial appointments seen not merely to uphold the Constitution but as tools to advance political agendas. The polarization surrounding judicial nominations has led to a crisis of confidence in the courts, with large segments of the population viewing decisions through the lens of political bias rather than legal principle.

The judiciary's vulnerability lies in the fact that it often operates in the shadows, away from the public eye, compared to the more visible branches of government. Courts do not wield the power of the purse like the legislature or command the military like the executive. Their power is derived from their legitimacy—the belief that they are impartial, fair, and committed to upholding the law. When that legitimacy is eroded, the entire legal system risks collapse.

- **Defending the Judiciary: A Call to Action**

The time to act is now. The judiciary cannot defend itself without the support of the public, legal professionals, and political leaders who believe in the fundamental principles of democracy. Citizens must recognize that judicial independence is not just an abstract concept; it is a tangible safeguard of their rights and freedoms. Without an independent judiciary, democracy itself is at risk.

One of the first steps in defending judicial independence is ensuring transparency in judicial processes. When courts are transparent in their decision-making and operate with open accountability, it becomes more difficult for those in power to manipulate them for political gain. Transparency allows the public to see that justice is being served, fostering trust in the institution.

Civil society must also play a critical role. Organizations that monitor judicial independence and advocate for the rule of law are essential to countering efforts to undermine the judiciary. These groups can bring attention to attacks on the judiciary and mobilize public support to defend it. In many countries where the judiciary has come under siege, it has been civil society organizations, legal scholars, and activists who have sounded the alarm and fought to preserve the integrity of the courts.

Another essential element of defending the judiciary is ensuring that judges themselves are empowered to maintain their independence. This requires robust protections for judges from political retaliation. Judges must be insulated from arbitrary removal or punishment based on their rulings. They should have the security of tenure, appropriate financial compensation, and clear ethical standards that guard against conflicts of interest. When judges know that they are protected from political retribution, they are more likely to make decisions based on law and conscience rather than fear of reprisal.

Furthermore, the media plays a vital role in shaping public perceptions of the judiciary. In a world where misinformation can spread rapidly, it is critical that the press provide accurate, balanced reporting on judicial decisions. Media outlets should resist sensationalism and instead focus on informing the public about the legal reasoning behind court rulings. A well-informed citizenry is less likely to fall prey to rhetoric that seeks to delegitimize the judiciary.

Political leaders, too, have a responsibility to defend the courts. Even when judicial rulings go against their policies or personal interests, it is crucial for leaders to uphold the legitimacy of the judiciary. This means resisting the temptation to attack judges or undermine court decisions through public rhetoric. Instead, political leaders should reaffirm their commitment to the rule of law and to the principle that no one is above it.

Lastly, international bodies and alliances, such as the United Nations, the European Union, and human rights organizations, must remain vigilant in defending judicial independence across the globe. When governments move to dismantle or politicize their courts, international pressure can be a powerful force in curbing these actions. Sanctions, diplomatic efforts, and public condemnations can help to deter authoritarian governments from further eroding the judiciary's independence.

- ## The Fragility of Justice

In the grand architecture of democracy, the judiciary is often viewed as the foundation—the bedrock that holds everything together. Yet, as we have seen, even the most solid foundations can be shaken. Judicial independence is not something that can be taken for granted. It must be constantly defended, nourished, and protected from those who seek to undermine it.

We are living in a time when the judiciary, once considered untouchable, is now under siege. The attacks may come in the form of legislative actions, public vilification, or even the subtle erosion of norms and ethics. But regardless of the form they take, these threats must be met with firm resistance.

The judiciary is not just a branch of government; it is the guardian of our rights, our freedoms, and our democracy. Without it, there can be no rule of law, and without the rule of law, there can be no democracy. The fight to defend judicial independence is, at its core, a fight to preserve the very essence of a free society.

As citizens, as advocates and as defenders of democracy, we must remain vigilant. The judiciary under siege is a call to action—a reminder that the price of justice is eternal vigilance. If we fail to act, we risk losing one of the most precious safeguards of our democratic way of life. If we rise to the challenge, we can ensure that the judiciary remains an impartial and independent force, dedicated to the protection of justice for all.

Chapter 9: Election Integrity: The Foundation of Democracy

In every democracy, the right to vote stands as the most fundamental principle upon which all other rights depend. Without the guarantee of free and fair elections, a society cannot call itself truly democratic. Election integrity is more than just a procedural formality—it is the very foundation upon which the legitimacy of governance is built. When citizens trust that their votes are counted accurately, their voices heard, and the electoral process is fair, they remain invested in the future of their country. However, when election integrity is undermined, either through outright manipulation or subtle forms of suppression, the legitimacy of the entire system comes into question.

- **Protecting the Vote: The Importance of Free and Fair Elections**

The promise of democracy is rooted in the simple but profound idea that the people have the right to choose their leaders. Every individual, regardless of wealth, status, or background, should have an equal say in the direction of their government. This principle was hard-fought throughout history, with suffrage movements, civil rights battles, and revolutions all pushing societies toward the recognition of universal voting rights. Protecting that right is essential to ensuring the continuation of a government by the people, for the people.

- **Why Free and Fair Elections Matter**

A free and fair election guarantees that citizens can cast their votes without fear of coercion or violence and that the results reflect the true will of the people. This process allows for a peaceful transfer of power, a hallmark of democratic stability. But more than that, elections serve as a moment for citizens to hold their leaders accountable, offering the chance to affirm or reject the policies and actions of their representatives.

Election integrity ensures that every citizen, regardless of geography, race, gender, or political affiliation, can exercise their democratic right. It fosters inclusivity, bringing different voices into the national conversation. In a society where elections are respected, there is an inherent recognition that while disagreements may exist, the collective will of the electorate holds primacy over individual ambitions or partisan desires.

The fight to protect the vote has not been easy. In many parts of the world, suffrage was initially reserved for the elite, often restricted by property ownership, gender, or race. The expansion of voting rights came only after sustained social pressure, political upheaval, and, in many cases, violent confrontation. The global suffrage movements of the 19th and 20th centuries, including women's suffrage and the struggle for racial equality, are a testament to the belief that voting is not a privilege—it is a fundamental human right.

In the United States, the Voting Rights Act of 1965 marked a turning point in the struggle to ensure that African Americans could exercise their right to vote. Prior to the act, discriminatory practices such as literacy tests, poll taxes, and outright intimidation were used to disenfranchise Black voters, especially in the southern states. The Voting Rights Act was instrumental in dismantling these barriers and safeguarding the integrity of elections. Yet, even after its passage, the battle to protect the vote continues, with new challenges arising that threaten to undermine this hard-won progress.

- **The Challenge of Integrity: Voter Suppression and Election Manipulation Tactics**

Despite the central importance of election integrity to the functioning of democracy, elections around the world have increasingly come under siege. From voter suppression tactics designed to disenfranchise marginalized groups to outright manipulation of election results, the threats to fair elections are varied and alarming.

- **Voter suppression: Silencing the electorate**

Voter suppression is one of the most insidious forms of undermining democracy. It occurs when laws, policies, or practices are put in place to make it more difficult for certain groups of people to vote. These tactics are often aimed at marginalized communities—ethnic minorities, the poor, the elderly, and young voters—who might be seen as less likely to support the status quo.

While ostensibly intended to prevent voter fraud, strict voter ID laws often disproportionately impact minority and low-income voters who may not have easy access to the required identification. In some countries, the requirements for obtaining an ID can be cumbersome, expensive, or inaccessible, effectively disenfranchising large portions of the population.

Another tactic involves the systematic removal of names from voter registration lists. While maintaining accurate voter rolls is important, the process of purging can often be mishandled, leading to the wrongful removal of legitimate voters. In some instances, individuals find out only on Election Day that they have been removed from the rolls, with little recourse.

"Gerrymandering" While not a direct form of voter suppression, gerrymandering—manipulating the boundaries of electoral districts to favor one party over another—can dilute the voting power of certain communities, particularly racial minorities. By drawing district lines in ways that concentrate or disperse voters strategically, those in power can ensure their continued dominance, regardless of the will of the electorate.

In some areas, particularly in poorer or rural communities, polling places are intentionally reduced or closed, making it difficult for voters to access a polling station. This can lead to long lines and excessive waiting times, discouraging people from voting, especially those who cannot afford to take time off work.

- **Eroding Trust In The System**

In addition to voter suppression, election manipulation presents a direct threat to democracy. Manipulation can take many forms, from tampering with vote counts to the spreading of misinformation designed to confuse or mislead voters. When voters cannot trust that their ballots are counted accurately or that election results reflect the true will of the people, faith in democracy begins to crumble.

One of the most significant threats to election integrity in the modern age comes from foreign interference. In recent years, cyberattacks, disinformation campaigns, and coordinated efforts to influence voters have emerged as sophisticated tools used to disrupt elections. Social media platforms have become battlegrounds where false information spreads rapidly, undermining confidence in the electoral process. Russia's interference in the 2016 U.S. presidential election, through a combination of hacking and disinformation, is a stark example of how vulnerable democratic processes can be to foreign actors.

A crucial, often overlooked, component of election integrity is public confidence in the system. Even when elections are technically free and fair, a concerted campaign of misinformation or baseless claims of fraud can convince significant portions of the population that the results are illegitimate. This is particularly dangerous in polarized societies, where mistrust in institutions is already high. When large segments of the electorate lose faith in the fairness of elections, it creates a volatile environment ripe for political unrest and authoritarianism.

The recent trend of leaders refusing to accept election results unless they win has created dangerous precedents. By casting doubt on the legitimacy of the electoral process, these leaders undermine democracy itself. This tactic not only destabilizes the immediate political environment but also has long-term consequences, eroding the very foundation of democratic governance.

- **The Path Forward: Securing Election Integrity**

Ensuring election integrity requires both vigilance and proactive measures. Democracies must take active steps to protect the vote from suppression and manipulation while fostering public trust in the electoral process.

Voter laws should aim to make voting more accessible, not less. Ensuring that every eligible citizen can vote without unnecessary barriers is a hallmark of a healthy democracy. This includes expanding early voting options, increasing the number of polling stations, and making voter registration as simple as possible. Additionally, measures like automatic voter registration and allowing same-day registration can help ensure that more people participate in the electoral process.

- **Combating Misinformation**

In the digital age, the fight for election integrity must also take place online. Social media platforms and tech companies have a responsibility to monitor and remove disinformation that can mislead voters. Fact-checking organizations must be supported and given prominence in public discourse. Public education campaigns that inform citizens about how to spot fake news and verify the accuracy of information are critical to creating a more informed electorate.

As cyber threats to elections continue to grow, nations must invest in robust cybersecurity measures to protect voting systems from hacking and tampering. Election infrastructure, from voter registration databases to electronic voting machines, must be secure, with regular audits to ensure accuracy and prevent fraud.

Perhaps the most difficult, yet most important, task is restoring public confidence in elections. This requires transparency in how elections are conducted and counted. Election observers, both domestic and international, should be present to verify the fairness of the process. Additionally, leaders must set a good example by accepting election results, even when they lose, and refraining from inflammatory rhetoric that undermines the integrity of the process.

Election integrity is the bedrock upon which all other democratic principles rest. Without the assurance that every vote counts and that the process is fair, citizens lose faith in the institutions meant to serve them. The challenges to election integrity—whether through voter suppression, manipulation, or foreign interference—are significant but not insurmountable. With vigilance, reform, and a commitment to truth, democracies can safeguard the electoral process and ensure that the voice of the people remains the ultimate authority.

As we move forward in a world where the forces of disinformation and authoritarianism are on the rise, the battle for election integrity will only become more critical. It is a fight not just for the right to vote but for the soul of democracy itself.

Chapter 10: The Media's Role in Democracy

The media is often called the "fourth estate," reflecting its power as a pillar of democracy alongside the executive, legislative, and judicial branches. It is the conduit through which information flows, holding those in power accountable and ensuring that citizens remain informed about the decisions and actions shaping their lives. In any healthy democracy, the media serves not merely as a passive observer but as an active participant, fostering public debate, promoting transparency, and protecting the rights of individuals. Without a free, independent press, democracy cannot truly thrive. The very nature of democracy relies on an informed populace capable of making educated decisions about the future of their society. In an age where misinformation spreads like wildfire and trust in the media has become increasingly fragile, the importance of a strong and independent press is more apparent than ever.

- **The Necessity of a Free and Independent Media in Holding Leaders Accountable**

At the heart of any functioning democracy lies the necessity of a free press. The ability of journalists to investigate, critique, and question authority without fear of retribution is foundational to ensuring that leaders remain accountable to the people. A free press is not just a privilege of democracy—it is a cornerstone of its integrity. When the press is restricted, controlled, or intimidated, the flow of information becomes polluted, leaving citizens in the dark and weakening the very foundations of governance.

- **Our Watchdog**

The media's role as a watchdog is one of its most vital functions. By shining a light on corruption, exposing abuses of power, and demanding transparency from those in authority, the press serves as a check on government excesses. Investigative journalism has uncovered scandals that have led to the resignation of high-ranking officials, the prosecution of criminals in power, and the reformation of unjust systems. From Watergate in the United States to the Panama Papers, the role of the media in exposing malfeasance is undeniable.

When the press is allowed to operate freely, it empowers citizens by keeping them informed of both the successes and failures of their leaders. A well-informed electorate is essential for holding public officials accountable, ensuring that they act in the public interest rather than for personal gain or power. When leaders know they are under scrutiny from a free and independent press, they are more likely to act with integrity, or at the very least, to think twice before engaging in unethical behavior.

- **Press Freedom and Human Rights**

The protection of a free press is intrinsically tied to the protection of human rights. Journalists often serve as the voice for the voiceless, reporting on issues such as poverty, discrimination, injustice, and abuse. Without the press, many human rights violations would go unnoticed, allowing perpetrators to act with impunity. In countries where the press is suppressed, dictatorships thrive, dissent is silenced, and abuses go unchecked.

Moreover, the press plays a key role in amplifying the concerns of marginalized communities, bringing attention to social issues that might otherwise be ignored. Whether it is reporting on racial discrimination, gender inequality, or environmental destruction, the media ensures that these issues receive the public attention they deserve. When the media is free to tell these stories, societies are better able to confront injustices and seek solutions.

Unfortunately, the freedom of the press is under threat in many parts of the world. Authoritarian regimes often view the media as a threat to their power and work tirelessly to undermine its independence. Journalists are frequently harassed, imprisoned, or even killed for daring to report on sensitive topics. In some cases, governments have enacted draconian laws aimed at silencing dissenting voices under the guise of national security or public order.

Even in democratic countries, the media faces increasing challenges. The rise of populist leaders has brought with it an antagonistic relationship with the press. Leaders who view critical media coverage as a personal attack often label the press as "the enemy of the people," undermining public trust in journalism and emboldening efforts to restrict press freedoms. This erosion of trust in the media, combined with the proliferation of "fake news" and disinformation, poses a serious threat to democracy itself.

- **Media Bias and Polarization: The Impact of Biased Reporting on Public Trust and Political Polarization**

While the necessity of a free press is undeniable, it is equally important to acknowledge that the media is not without its own challenges. In recent years, concerns over media bias and its role in exacerbating political polarization have come to the forefront of public debate. As societies become increasingly divided along ideological lines, the media often finds itself both a symptom and a driver of this polarization.

Media bias is not a new phenomenon. Historically, newspapers and other media outlets have often aligned themselves with political parties or ideologies. However, the advent of 24-hour news channels and the rise of digital media have amplified the effects of media bias in ways previously unimaginable. Today, many media outlets cater to specific ideological audiences, reinforcing pre-existing beliefs rather than challenging them. This selective reporting leads to a fractured media landscape where citizens consume news that confirms their biases, creating echo chambers that distort reality.

When media outlets present news through a partisan lens, it becomes increasingly difficult for citizens to engage with facts objectively. Instead of receiving balanced coverage, audiences are fed narratives designed to appeal to their emotions and political leanings. This not only diminishes the quality of public debate but also erodes trust in the media. People begin to view the news not as a source of truth but as a tool of political manipulation, further deepening divisions within society.

- **Polarization and the Erosion of Civil Discourse**

The impact of media bias is perhaps most evident in the growing polarization that characterizes many democracies today. When citizens only consume media that aligns with their beliefs, they become more entrenched in their views and less willing to engage in constructive dialogue with those who hold opposing opinions. This leads to a breakdown in civil discourse, where disagreement is no longer seen as an opportunity for debate but as a threat to one's identity.

In highly polarized societies, the media plays a central role in fueling the divide. News outlets that prioritize sensationalism and conflict over thoughtful analysis contribute to an environment where the "us versus them" mentality dominates public discourse. This, in turn, fosters a culture of hostility and mistrust, making it increasingly difficult for citizens to find common ground.

- **The Echo Chamber Effect**

The rise of social media has further complicated the media's role in democracy. Platforms like Facebook, Twitter, and YouTube have become primary sources of news for millions of people around the world. However, these platforms are designed to prioritize content that generates engagement, often favoring sensationalist or emotionally charged material over balanced reporting.

Social media algorithms create echo chambers by showing users content that aligns with their preferences, reinforcing existing beliefs, and filtering out dissenting opinions. This echo chamber effect not only deepens polarization but also makes it easier for misinformation to spread unchecked. When people are constantly exposed to news that affirms their worldview, they become less likely to question the accuracy of the information they consume, making them more vulnerable to false or misleading narratives.

The decline in public trust in the media is a troubling trend that must be addressed if democracy is to flourish. To restore trust, media outlets must prioritize transparency, accountability, and impartiality in their reporting. Journalists must commit to rigorous fact-checking, avoid sensationalism, and strive to present a balanced view of events, even when it is unpopular or uncomfortable.

In addition, the media must take responsibility for the role it plays in shaping public opinion. Rather than catering to ideological audiences, news organizations should aim to foster informed debate and encourage critical thinking. By presenting multiple perspectives and providing context for complex issues, the media can help bridge the divide between polarized factions and promote a more nuanced understanding of the world.

- **The Media as a Bridge and Not a Barrier**

Despite the challenges posed by bias and polarization, the media has the potential to be a force for unity rather than division. When used responsibly, the media can foster dialogue, bridge divides, and promote understanding among diverse communities. Rather than amplifying conflict, the media can play a crucial role in helping societies navigate differences and find common ground.

One of the most effective ways to combat the negative effects of media bias and polarization is through media literacy education. Citizens must be equipped with the tools to critically analyze the news they consume, question the credibility of sources, and recognize bias when it appears. By fostering a more media-literate populace, societies can reduce the influence of sensationalist or biased reporting and promote a more informed and engaged electorate.

- **The Role of Independent Journalism**

Independent journalism is more important than ever in today's polarized media landscape. Independent news organizations, free from corporate or government influence, provide a vital counterbalance to the sensationalism and partisanship that characterize much of mainstream media. These outlets often prioritize investigative reporting, shining a light on stories that might otherwise go unreported.

Supporting independent journalism is essential for ensuring that the media remains a force for good in society. Citizens, policymakers, and businesses alike must recognize the value of independent journalism and invest in its continued existence. In doing so, they help ensure that the media remains a powerful tool for truth, accountability, and democracy.

The media plays an irreplaceable role in any democracy. It is the primary mechanism by which citizens remain informed about the actions of their leaders and the state of their nation. A free and independent press is essential for holding those in power accountable and ensuring that democratic principles are upheld. Without it, the people are left in the dark, and democracy is weakened.

As we move forward, the task is clear: protect the independence of the press, hold it to high standards of integrity, and empower citizens with the tools to critically engage with the information they consume. Only then can we ensure that the media remains a foundation of democracy, helping to inform, unite, and empower the people it serves.

Chapter 11: Global Democracy at a Crossroad

Democracy, as a system of governance, has long been revered as the pinnacle of human political evolution. It offers freedom, participation, and a government by the people for the people. Yet, in the 21st century, this ideal is increasingly under threat. The world is at a crossroads, where the principles that have defined democracies across the globe are being tested, strained, and, in some cases, dismantled. As we explore the nuances of this moment in history, it is essential to recognize that the challenges facing democracy in the United States are not unique. Across continents and political systems, many countries are grappling with populism, authoritarianism, erosion of trust in institutions, and the polarization of public discourse. What we witness today is not just an American crisis; it is a global crisis, one that demands attention, reflection, and action.

- **How the American Experience Mirrors Global Trends in Democratic Decline**

The decline of democracy in the United States is part of a wider trend that has gripped democracies worldwide. The same forces that have contributed to the erosion of democratic norms in the U.S.—polarization, misinformation, populism and attacks on institutions—are visible in other countries as well. This is not coincidental but rather symptomatic of deeper, global trends that are reshaping the political landscape.

One of the most alarming parallels between the United States and other nations experiencing democratic decline is the rise of political polarization. In many democratic countries, the center ground of politics has all but disappeared, replaced by increasingly extreme positions on both the left and right. This polarization, fueled by populist rhetoric, has fragmented societies and made it harder for people to find common ground.

In the U.S., we see this polarization in every facet of public life, from Congress to everyday conversations. Political discourse has become so divided that compromise is seen as betrayal, and bipartisan cooperation has become nearly impossible. The same phenomenon is visible in other democracies, where political parties once united by common values now cater to niche, ideologically driven bases. Countries such as Brazil, India, and Hungary are all grappling with the divisive politics that fragment their societies, drawing people away from the middle ground and into opposing camps.

This polarization is not limited to political institutions; it seeps into communities, families, and even friendships. In polarized societies, people increasingly live in ideological silos, consuming news and interacting with people who share their views. This creates echo chambers where misinformation spreads unchecked, and dissenting opinions are seen not as different viewpoints but as attacks on one's identity.

- **Populism and the Rise of Authoritarianism**

Another significant trend that parallels the American experience is the rise of populist leaders who exploit discontent, fear, and anger to gain power. These leaders often present themselves as the voice of "the people," claiming to challenge corrupt elites and speak on behalf of the "forgotten." However, beneath this rhetoric lies a more dangerous agenda—an erosion of democratic norms, an assault on institutions, and a concentration of power in the hands of the executive.

In the United States, this trend has been particularly visible in recent years, where populist rhetoric has been used to delegitimize elections, attack the press, and undermine the judiciary. The playbook of populism is clear: create an "us versus them" narrative, scapegoat marginalized groups, and cast doubt on the legitimacy of democratic institutions. This same playbook is being used in other countries, where populist leaders have similarly attacked the foundations of democracy.

In Turkey, for example, President Recep Tayyip Erdoğan has consolidated power over two decades, systematically weakening democratic institutions. By controlling the media, suppressing dissent, and manipulating the judiciary, Erdoğan has transformed Turkey from a democracy into a semi-authoritarian regime. A similar story can be told in Hungary, where Prime Minister Viktor Orbán has undermined democratic institutions while promoting an exclusionary, nationalist vision of "illiberal democracy." In Brazil, former President Jair Bolsonaro's populist approach destabilized trust in democratic processes, with claims of voter fraud that mirrored American political discourse in recent elections.

Populism has a dangerous consequence: it weakens the very institutions that protect democracy from authoritarianism. By attacking the press, the judiciary, and legislative bodies, populist leaders hollow out the checks and balances that are essential to preserving democratic governance. The result is often the rise of autocracy in the guise of democracy, where leaders claim a mandate from "the people" while systematically dismantling democratic norms.

- **Erosion of Trust in Institutions**

Trust in democratic institutions is the bedrock of any functioning democracy. In the United States, we have witnessed a gradual erosion of this trust, particularly in recent years. The courts, the media, law enforcement, and even the electoral process itself have all been subject to unprecedented scrutiny and attacks. When trust in these institutions erodes, it weakens democracy's foundation, making it vulnerable to manipulation and abuse.

This erosion of trust is not unique to the U.S. In Poland, the ruling Law and Justice Party has pushed through judicial reforms that effectively bring the courts under political control, sparking massive protests and EU sanctions. In India, the world's largest democracy, trust in the judiciary has also been tested under Prime Minister Narendra Modi, whose government has been accused of undermining the rule of law. In countries like the Philippines under President

Rodrigo Duterte, public confidence in law enforcement and the judiciary has plummeted due to extrajudicial killings and government-sanctioned human rights abuses.

Around the world, citizens are growing disillusioned with their governments and institutions. This disillusionment creates fertile ground for authoritarianism as citizens, frustrated with the failures of democracy, become more willing to accept strongman rule in exchange for stability and order. The erosion of trust feeds the narrative that democracy is broken, leading to calls for drastic change that often involve a move away from democratic principles.

- **Lessons from Other Countries Facing Similar Challenges**

To understand the challenges faced by democracies worldwide, it is essential to look at specific case studies. Each of these countries offers important lessons about the fragility of democracy, the consequences of democratic backsliding, and the potential paths toward recovery.

- **Hungary: The Case of Illiberal Democracy**

Hungary under Prime Minister Viktor Orbán represents a clear case of how democracy can be hollowed out from within. Orbán came to power in 2010, and over the subsequent years, he has systematically dismantled democratic institutions while maintaining the appearance of democracy. His government has rewritten the constitution, undermined the independence of the judiciary, and taken control of much of the media.

Orbán's brand of "illiberal democracy" is based on the idea that democracy should serve the interests of the nation, defined in exclusionary, often ethnic terms. Under his leadership, Hungary has seen a sharp rise in nationalism and anti-immigrant rhetoric, with civil society organizations coming under attack. While elections are still held, they are not truly free or fair, as opposition parties struggle to compete in an environment where the media and institutions are controlled by the ruling party.

Hungary offers a sobering lesson: democratic backsliding can occur even within the structures of democracy. When leaders manipulate institutions for personal gain and weaken the checks and balances that protect democracy, the system itself becomes fragile.

- **Brazil: Populism and Disinformation**

Brazil, under former President Jair Bolsonaro, illustrates the dangers of populism combined with widespread disinformation. Bolsonaro's rise to power was fueled by a wave of populist anger, much of it driven by the perception that the country's political elites were corrupt and out of touch with the people. Once in office, Bolsonaro followed the populist playbook: attacking the media, undermining democratic institutions, and casting doubt on the legitimacy of the electoral process.

In the 2022 elections, Bolsonaro repeatedly claimed that the electoral system was rigged against him, leading to widespread protests and concerns about potential violence. While he ultimately left office after losing to President Luiz Inácio Lula da Silva, the damage done to Brazil's democratic institutions is significant. Bolsonaro's rhetoric has sown deep distrust in the electoral process, with millions of Brazilians now questioning the legitimacy of their democracy.

Brazil's experience highlights the dangers of disinformation in undermining democratic norms. When leaders spread falsehoods about the electoral process, they erode public confidence in democracy itself, making it harder to restore trust even after they leave office.

- **The Philippines: Strongman Rule and Human Rights**

Under President Rodrigo Duterte, the Philippines has experienced a dramatic erosion of democratic norms. Duterte's war on drugs, marked by extrajudicial killings and widespread human rights abuses, has shocked the world. Yet, Duterte's populist rhetoric, framed around the need for security and order, has resonated with large segments of the Filipino population.

Duterte's rule demonstrates the dangers of prioritizing order over freedom. In the name of fighting crime, Duterte has weakened the judiciary, attacked the press, and consolidated power in the executive. While his popularity remains high among certain groups, his presidency has left a legacy of human rights abuses and weakened democratic institutions that will take years to repair.

The lesson from the Philippines is clear: when strongman leaders prioritize power over democratic principles, the cost to society is immense. Human rights are often the first casualty, followed by the erosion of trust in institutions that are meant to protect the people.

As we reflect on the global state of democracy, it is evident that the challenges facing the United States are not isolated. Around the world, democracies are at a crossroads, with many nations grappling with similar issues of polarization, populism, and the erosion of trust in institutions. The rise of authoritarianism, disinformation, and the weakening of democratic norms are trends that transcend borders, affecting countries in every region of the world.

However, this moment also offers an opportunity. The lessons from other countries provide a roadmap for how democracies can resist backsliding and renew their commitment to the principles of freedom, justice, and equality. The American experience, with all its challenges, can serve as a cautionary tale but also as a source of hope. Democracy, though fragile, is resilient. It requires constant vigilance, but it also has the capacity for renewal and reform.

The road ahead is not easy, but it is clear: the global community must come together to defend democracy at this critical juncture. By learning from the experiences of other countries and working to restore trust in democratic institutions, we can chart a path forward that ensures democracy remains a vital force for good in the world.

Chapter 12: The Rise of Authoritarianism: A Global Threat

The struggle between authoritarianism and democracy has become one of the defining global battles of our time. Across continents, authoritarian regimes have gained ground, using a combination of fear, manipulation, and suppression to consolidate power. At the same time, democracy—long considered the bedrock of free societies—has come under threat even in countries where it was once seen as invulnerable.

Let's narrow it down to see the complex relationship between authoritarianism and democracy. It explores not just the growing threat posed by authoritarian leaders but also the need for a global, unified response to safeguard democratic ideals. The rise of authoritarianism is not just a problem for individual countries—it is a global phenomenon that demands a global solution.

- **Authoritarianism vs. Democracy: A Global Struggle**

In recent years, authoritarian leaders have found ways to chip away at the democratic institutions meant to keep them in check. They have exploited weaknesses in electoral systems, manipulated public opinion, and undermined the independence of the judiciary and the media. These actions are often justified under the guise of maintaining "order" or "national security," but the true goal is almost always the same: the consolidation of power in the hands of a few.

What makes this threat particularly dangerous is its global nature. Authoritarianism is not confined to any one region of the world. From Eastern Europe to South America, from Asia to Africa, leaders with autocratic tendencies have risen to power by appealing to nationalism, stoking fears of outsiders, and presenting themselves as the only solution to their countries' problems. Their playbook is strikingly similar: they challenge the legitimacy of elections, crackdown on dissent, and vilify the free press, all while framing themselves as protectors of their nation's sovereignty and cultural identity.

The threat authoritarianism poses to democracy is not just internal; it also extends beyond borders. These regimes often seek to destabilize neighboring democracies or influence international organizations. The result is a domino effect—when one democracy falls or weakens, others become more vulnerable. This is particularly evident in how authoritarian regimes support one another, both diplomatically and financially, creating a network of repression that stretches across continents.

Consider the tactics of contemporary authoritarian regimes. They use the legal system as a weapon, charging political opponents with fabricated crimes while dismantling checks and balances that are essential for any functioning democracy. In countries like Hungary, Russia, and Turkey, we have witnessed the gradual erosion of democracy under the guise of "reforms" that ultimately serve to strengthen the grip of power-hungry leaders. In other cases, such as Venezuela or Belarus, elections have become mere formalities, where outcomes are predetermined and opposition candidates are either imprisoned or forced into exile.

This creeping authoritarianism is not limited to traditionally fragile democracies. Even in more established democracies, we have seen worrying trends—such as political leaders questioning the legitimacy of elections, undermining the independence of the judiciary, or leveraging social media to stoke division. The rise of populist movements in countries like the United States, the United Kingdom, and Brazil has further contributed to the erosion of democratic norms, as leaders who embrace autocratic tendencies gain power by appealing to fears and prejudices.

The challenge of authoritarianism is not just that it dismantles democratic institutions; it is also that it redefines the political discourse and norms. Authoritarian leaders thrive on division and fear, weaponizing these emotions to silence dissent and control public opinion. By painting themselves as saviors in times of crisis, they justify their increasingly autocratic actions and persuade segments of the population to trade their democratic freedoms for the promise of security and stability. Yet history has shown us time and again that the price of such a bargain is too high.

The rise of authoritarianism is not only a threat to individual countries—it poses a significant risk to global stability. Authoritarian leaders often adopt an aggressive foreign policy, seeking to expand their influence beyond their borders through military intervention, cyberattacks, or political interference. Their disregard for international norms and laws undermines global institutions designed to promote peace and cooperation, making the world a more dangerous and unstable place.

Russia's annexation of Crimea in 2014 and its ongoing military involvement in Ukraine, for example, was not only a blatant violation of international law but also a symbol of how authoritarian leaders are willing to disrupt global order to achieve their aims. The rise of China as a global superpower has also raised concerns, particularly as the Chinese government tightens its control domestically and flexes its muscles on the international stage, seeking to reshape global institutions in ways that favor authoritarian governance.

In an interconnected world, the impact of authoritarianism reverberates far beyond the borders of the countries in which it takes root. It weakens alliances, disrupts trade, and fuels conflict as authoritarian regimes seek to expand their influence and undermine the global democratic order. If left unchecked, the spread of authoritarianism could lead to a world where democracy is the exception rather than the rule and where international norms that have fostered cooperation and peace are replaced by a system driven by power and fear.

- **Global Solidarity**

In the face of the growing authoritarian threat, it is imperative that democracies around the world stand together. The fight for democracy is not just a national issue—it is a global one.

Authoritarian leaders have shown that they are willing to collaborate and support each other in their efforts to suppress dissent and undermine democratic norms. To counter this, democracies must also come together in defense of shared values.

Global solidarity begins with recognizing that the fight for democracy is interconnected. What happens in one part of the world affects us all. When a democracy is eroded in Eastern Europe, it sends ripples across the globe, emboldening authoritarian leaders elsewhere to follow suit. When a free press is silenced in Southeast Asia, it weakens the global push for transparency and accountability. If we are to successfully combat the rise of authoritarianism, we must recognize that the defense of democracy is a collective responsibility.

International cooperation is essential in defending democracy. Democratic nations must use their influence in global organizations like the United Nations, the European Union, and the Organization of American States to hold authoritarian regimes accountable. Sanctions, diplomatic pressure, and other tools of foreign policy must be employed to send a clear message: the world will not stand idly by while democracy is dismantled.

Supporting democratic movements within authoritarian regimes is another key component of global solidarity. From Hong Kong to Belarus, we have seen courageous citizens rise in defense of their freedoms, often at great personal risk. These movements need support from the international community—whether through financial assistance, safe havens for dissidents, or platforms to amplify their voices. The battle for democracy must be fought not just by governments but by civil society as well.

Global solidarity also means reaffirming the values of democracy at home, and in our case, "America." Democracies must lead by example, ensuring that their own institutions remain strong, transparent, and accountable. It is not enough to condemn authoritarianism abroad while ignoring the erosion of democratic norms within our own borders. By upholding democratic values and addressing the internal challenges facing our democracies—whether it be political polarization, economic inequality, or misinformation—we can demonstrate to the world that democracy is not only worth defending but is also capable of delivering on its promises.

- **The Importance of International Cooperation**

In defending democracy against authoritarianism, international cooperation is not just beneficial—it is essential. No nation can confront this threat on its own. The rise of authoritarianism has shown us that the challenges we face are not confined by geography. Cyberattacks, misinformation campaigns, and economic coercion are all tools used by authoritarian regimes to weaken democratic societies. Countering these tactics requires a coordinated global effort.

Through international alliances, democratic nations can pool their resources and expertise to confront the unique challenges posed by authoritarianism. By sharing intelligence, coordinating sanctions, and promoting democratic norms, democracies can push back against the global tide of authoritarianism. But it requires more than just government action—civil society organizations, the private sector, and individuals all have a role to play in defending democracy.

The rise of authoritarianism represents one of the most significant challenges to global democracy in the modern era. As authoritarian leaders undermine democratic institutions and erode the rule of law, the very principles of freedom, equality, and justice are at stake. This is not just a national battle but a global one, and the future of democracy depends on our collective response.

The fight against authoritarianism will be long and difficult, but it is one worth waging. By standing together in global solidarity, supporting democratic movements, and reaffirming our commitment to democratic values, we can push back against the forces of authoritarianism and ensure that democracy prevails.

The road ahead is uncertain, but history has shown that when people unite in defense of their freedoms, even the most entrenched autocracies can be dismantled. Democracy may be under siege, but it is not defeated. With global cooperation and unwavering resolve, we can safeguard democracy for future generations and create a world where freedom and justice triumph over tyranny and repression.

Chapter 13: Lessons from the Past: Avoiding the Mistakes of History

History often serves as both a mirror and a warning. For every democratic system that thrives, there are countless examples of those that faltered, collapsed, or were dismantled by authoritarian forces. The arc of human civilization is filled with stories of progress, yet it is also riddled with instances of backsliding, where nations allowed democratic institutions to weaken under pressure or manipulation.

This chapter looks back to learn from the past, drawing lessons from the rise and fall of previous democracies. These lessons are not mere academic reflections but urgent warnings for the present. If we fail to heed the past, we risk repeating the same mistakes, and the consequences could be devastating, not only for individual nations but for global democracy itself.

- **Historical Parallels: Lessons from Past Democracies that Fell to Authoritarianism**

Throughout history, we see numerous examples of democracies that succumbed to authoritarianism, often through a combination of internal strife, external threats, and the calculated manipulation of power. These lessons provide clear parallels to the challenges we face today.

One of the most famous historical examples is the fall of the Roman Republic, a system that, much like today's democracies, prided itself on a balance of power, rule of law, and a participatory form of governance. Yet, over time, the Roman Republic eroded from within. Economic inequality widened, political corruption flourished, and populist leaders exploited divisions within society. The republic gradually gave way to autocratic rule, leading to the eventual rise of emperors like Julius Caesar and Augustus, who effectively dismantled the democratic system. The collapse of the Roman Republic serves as a powerful reminder that no democracy, no matter how strong, is immune to internal decay.

Another significant example comes from the Weimar Republic in Germany. Established in the wake of World War I, the Weimar Republic represented a fragile democratic experiment in a country that had long been dominated by authoritarian monarchy. The republic was plagued by economic hardship, political extremism, and a lack of faith in its institutions. Adolf Hitler's rise to power through democratic means, followed by his swift consolidation of power into a fascist dictatorship, highlights how easily democracies can fall when authoritarian leaders exploit crises to manipulate public opinion. The Weimar Republic's fall shows how fragile democracy can be in the face of economic instability and extremist rhetoric.

Further east, in Russia, the early 20th century provides another stark parallel. After the Russian Revolution of 1917, the fledgling Russian democracy was crushed under the weight of internal conflict, economic turmoil, and political infighting. The Bolsheviks, led by Lenin, promised stability and progress but instead ushered in decades of authoritarian rule under Soviet Communism. Here, too, we see how democratic aspirations can be subverted when authoritarian figures seize upon societal unrest to solidify their power.

Latin America offers yet more examples. In the mid-20th century, countries like Argentina, Chile, and Brazil experienced military coups that toppled democratic governments. In many cases, these coups were justified under the pretense of restoring "order" in the face of political instability or economic crises. In Chile, Salvador Allende's government was democratically elected, but his socialist policies and increasing polarization made him a target for a military coup led by General Augusto Pinochet. The coup marked the end of Chile's democracy and the beginning of a brutal dictatorship, where human rights abuses and political repression became the norm. The lesson here is clear: democracies are often most vulnerable in times of division and crisis.

These historical examples are not relics of the distant past but warnings for today. The common thread among them is that the decline of democracy often starts not with a sudden revolution but with gradual, incremental steps. Leaders slowly chip away at democratic norms, using crises—whether economic, political, or social—as pretexts for their actions. Public trust in institutions erodes, political discourse becomes polarized, and before long, democracy gives way to autocracy.

The key takeaway from these historical parallels is that democracy is fragile. It requires constant vigilance, public engagement, and a commitment to democratic principles, even in the face of adversity. The moment we take democracy for granted is the moment it becomes most vulnerable.

If history has taught us anything, it is that democracy can fail when citizens, leaders, and institutions become complacent. To prevent the mistakes of the past from repeating themselves, we must learn from those moments where democracies faltered and take active steps to safeguard against similar outcomes.

First, it is essential to protect the integrity of democratic institutions. Whether it is the judiciary, the legislative branch, or the electoral system, these institutions must remain independent and free from manipulation. Historical examples show that when leaders begin undermining the judiciary or attempting to circumvent constitutional processes, democracy is on dangerous ground. The United States, for example, has faced challenges to judicial independence in recent years, with political pressure threatening to erode the impartiality of the courts. If the rule of law is to be upheld, judicial independence must be fiercely protected.

Second, fostering a culture of democratic engagement is crucial. One of the greatest threats to democracy is public apathy. When citizens disengage from the political process, authoritarian leaders find it easier to erode democratic norms. History shows that authoritarian regimes often rise when large segments of the population feel disillusioned or disconnected from the political process, making them more susceptible to extremist rhetoric. To prevent this, we must ensure that citizens are actively involved in democracy, not only during elections but in the ongoing civic process. Civic education, political participation, and public dialogue are the lifeblood of a healthy democracy.

Third, it is vital to resist the temptation of populism and demagoguery. Authoritarian leaders often rise by presenting themselves as outsiders, claiming to represent "the people" against a corrupt elite. This rhetoric, while appealing in times of crisis, is dangerous because it encourages the erosion of checks and balances. Leaders who position themselves as saviors often seek to concentrate power in their hands, bypassing democratic processes in the name of expediency. To avoid falling into this trap, societies must foster political discourse that values debate, compromise, and the rule of law over the false promise of quick, authoritarian fixes.

Fourth, economic inequality must be addressed. Many of the historical examples of democratic collapse occurred in the context of severe economic hardship. When wealth and power become concentrated in the hands of a few while large segments of the population struggle to meet basic needs, democracy is at risk. Economic inequality breeds resentment, and that resentment can be easily exploited by authoritarian leaders. As a result, it is essential to promote policies that create a more equitable society, where all citizens have a stake in the democratic process.

Fifth, the media must be free and independent, providing citizens with accurate information and serving as a watchdog against government overreach. One of the commonalities among failed democracies is the suppression or co-opting of the press. When the media is silenced or manipulated, authoritarian leaders can operate with impunity. Democracies today face the added challenge of disinformation, which has the potential to distort public opinion and undermine democratic legitimacy. Protecting press freedom and ensuring the public has access to reliable information is critical to maintaining a healthy democracy.

Finally, international solidarity is crucial. Just as authoritarian regimes often collaborate, democracies must also support each other. This means defending democratic principles not only within our own borders but also on the global stage. When authoritarian leaders rise in one country, the international community must respond swiftly and decisively. Inaction or appeasement only emboldens authoritarian figures, as seen in the lead-up to World War II when European democracies hesitated to confront the rising fascist regimes of Germany and Italy. Collective action is essential in preventing the spread of authoritarianism.

- **A Future Guided by the Past**

The history of democracy is one of both triumph and tragedy. While democracy has been one of the greatest achievements of human civilization, its survival is never guaranteed. As this chapter demonstrates, the fall of past democracies provides invaluable lessons for the present and the future. By learning from the mistakes of history, we can better equip ourselves to defend democracy in the face of growing challenges.

The past warns us that democracy can be fragile, easily undermined by complacency, inequality, and extremism. But it also shows us that the fight for democracy is worth fighting. When citizens, leaders, and institutions come together to defend democratic principles, democracy can be strengthened, even in the most difficult of times.

As we look to the future, we must remember that the fate of democracy rests in our hands. By fostering a culture of civic engagement, protecting democratic institutions, resisting populism, and promoting economic justice, we can build a future where democracy not only survives but thrives. The past has shown us the consequences of inaction—now, it is up to us to chart a different course, especially in the coming election. A decision that is guided by the hard-earned lessons of history.

Chapter 14: A Blueprint for Democratic Comeback

The strength of a democracy lies not in its perfection but in its capacity for renewal and reform. Like any living organism, democracy must adapt and evolve to meet the challenges of the times and trends. History teaches us those periods of democratic decline often precede moments of renewal—when citizens, leaders, and institutions come together to revitalize the democratic experiment. As we face an era of rising authoritarianism and increasing polarization, the need for democratic reforms has never been more urgent.

Let's x-ray the outlines of a blueprint for a democratic comeback—a roadmap that suggests key reforms and strategies to fortify democratic institutions, protect the integrity of the political system, and build resilience against authoritarian threats. The blueprint is not a quick fix but a long-term vision that will require sustained effort, civic engagement, and a commitment to the principles of democracy. The lessons of history have shown us what happens when democracies fail; now is the time to forge a new path forward.

- **Reform Proposals: Strengthening Democratic Institutions**

Democratic institutions are the bedrock of any functioning democracy, yet they are vulnerable to manipulation, corruption, and erosion from within. To ensure the long-term health of democracy, we must strengthen these institutions with a series of targeted reforms designed to make them more transparent, accountable, and responsive to the needs of the people.

1. **Electoral Reform: Protecting the Integrity of the Vote**

The integrity of elections is fundamental to the legitimacy of any democracy. Yet, in recent years, many democracies around the world have faced challenges to election integrity, from gerrymandering and voter suppression to the spread of disinformation and cyber interference. Reforming the electoral system is the first step toward a democratic resurgence.

One of the most pressing reforms is the implementation of independent, non-partisan redistricting commissions to combat gerrymandering. Gerrymandering, the manipulation of electoral district boundaries for political gain, undermines the principle of fair representation. By drawing district lines in ways that favor one political party, it distorts the democratic process and allows politicians to choose their voters rather than the other way around. Independent commissions, free from political influence, should be tasked with drawing electoral maps that reflect genuine demographic and geographic realities, ensuring that every vote counts equally.

Another essential reform is expanding access to the vote. Voter suppression tactics, whether through restrictive voter ID laws, purging voter rolls, or limiting early voting, have disenfranchised millions of voters, particularly minority communities. Ensuring that every eligible citizen can vote must be a priority. Automatic voter registration, expanded early voting, and measures to make voting more accessible, such as mail-in ballots or making Election Day a national holiday, are crucial steps in this direction. These reforms would reduce barriers to voting and enhance participation, making elections more inclusive and representative.

2. **Campaign Finance Reform**

Money has long played a corrosive role in democratic politics. The outsized influence of wealthy donors and corporate interests has skewed the political process in favor of the few at the expense of the many. To strengthen democracy, we must limit the role of money in politics and ensure that the voices of ordinary citizens are not drowned out by those with deep pockets.

A key reform in this area is the implementation of public financing for campaigns. By providing candidates with public funds for their campaigns, we can reduce their dependence on private donations and corporate interests. This would allow candidates to focus on representing their constituents rather than catering to the demands of their largest donors. Moreover, public financing would level the playing field, making it easier for candidates from diverse backgrounds to run for office, thereby enhancing the democratic process.

In addition to public financing, greater transparency in campaign contributions is essential. Dark money—political spending by undisclosed donors—undermines accountability and erodes public trust in the political system. Laws that require full disclosure of political donations, as well as limits on the amount individuals and corporations can contribute, are necessary to restore faith in democracy.

3. **Media Reform**

A free and independent press is one of the cornerstones of democracy, but the modern media landscape is fraught with challenges. The rise of partisan media, the proliferation of disinformation, and the consolidation of media ownership have all contributed to the erosion of public trust in the media. To strengthen democracy, we must ensure that the press remains a reliable source of information and a watchdog against government abuses.

One proposal is to support public-interest journalism through public funding or tax incentives. Independent journalism, particularly investigative reporting, plays a crucial role in holding leaders accountable and exposing corruption. However, the financial pressures facing traditional media outlets have led to a decline in investigative journalism, particularly at the local level. Providing public funding for independent journalism can help restore the media's role as a check on power and an essential part of democratic discourse.

Media literacy education is another critical reform. In an era of disinformation and fake news, it is vital that citizens are equipped with the tools to critically evaluate the information they consume. Media literacy programs should be incorporated into school curricula, teaching young people how to identify reliable sources, discern fact from opinion, and recognize the tactics used to spread false information. An informed electorate is the backbone of a healthy democracy, and media literacy is a key component of building that foundation.

- **Defending Democracy from Authoritarian Threats**

As we implement reforms to strengthen democratic institutions, we must also focus on building resilience within these institutions to withstand authoritarian threats. History shows that authoritarianism often takes root when democratic institutions are weak or compromised. To prevent this, we must create structures that are resistant to manipulation and ensure that power remains accountable to the people.

1. **Protecting the Rule of Law**

An independent judiciary is crucial for maintaining the rule of law and safeguarding individual rights. However, authoritarian leaders often seek to undermine the judiciary, stacking courts with loyalists or attacking judges who rule against them. To safeguard democracy, judicial independence must be preserved at all costs.

One key reform is implementing merit-based judicial appointments. Instead of allowing political leaders to appoint judges based on partisan considerations, independent commissions should be tasked with selecting judges based on their qualifications and commitment to the rule of law. This would help ensure that the judiciary remains impartial and insulated from political pressures.

Term limits for judges, particularly on higher courts, are another proposal to prevent the judiciary from becoming overly politicized. Lifetime appointments, while intended to protect judicial independence, can lead to entrenched ideologies and a lack of accountability. Implementing reasonable term limits would strike a balance between independence and accountability, ensuring a judiciary that remains dynamic and responsive to societal changes while remaining committed to the principles of justice.

2. **Civic Education: Engaging Citizens in the Democratic Process**

A resilient democracy depends on an engaged and informed citizenry. When citizens understand how their government works and their role within it, they are better equipped to defend democratic institutions from authoritarian encroachment. Civic education is essential for fostering this kind of engagement.

Comprehensive civic education should be a priority at all levels of schooling. Students must learn not only the mechanics of government but also the values that underpin democracy—freedom, equality, justice, and the rule of law. They should be taught the importance of participation in the political process, from voting to activism, and how to critically evaluate the information they receive. Civic education should also emphasize the importance of compromise and dialogue in a democracy, helping to bridge the divisions that often lead to polarization and extremism.

In addition to formal education, civic engagement programs aimed at adults can help build a more informed and active electorate. Community forums, voter education initiatives, and public discussions on democratic principles can foster a culture of participation that strengthens democracy from the ground up.

- **A Democratic Revival**

The path to a democratic comeback is neither easy nor swift, but it is possible. The reforms outlined in this chapter represent a roadmap for strengthening democratic institutions, restoring public trust, and building resilience against authoritarian threats. While no single reform can solve the complex challenges facing democracy, taken together, they offer a comprehensive strategy for renewal.

At the heart of this blueprint is the idea that democracy is not a static system but a dynamic process that requires constant care and adaptation. It is up to all of us—citizens, leaders, and institutions—to defend and strengthen democracy for future generations.

The road ahead will require courage, commitment, and a belief in the power of collective action. But if history has shown us anything, it is that democracy can endure, even in the face of its greatest challenges, when people are willing to fight for it. The democratic comeback begins now.

Chapter 15: The Responsibility of Citizenship

At the heart of every democracy lies its most vital force: **the citizens themselves**. Governments may legislate, institutions may safeguard rights, and leaders may guide nations, but ultimately, it is the collective power of the people that sustains and nurtures democratic life. Without an engaged and informed citizenry, no number of institutional safeguards can protect a democracy from decay. Democracy, by its very nature, demands active participation, vigilance, and a deep commitment to the common good.

A functioning democracy is not just a matter of elections or government institutions but an ongoing dialogue between citizens and their representatives. The health of democracy depends on citizens willingness to engage, to question, and to hold their leaders accountable. It also rests on the capacity of individuals to understand the civic duties that come with freedom as well as the importance of educating future generations on these responsibilities.

- **The Lifeblood of Democracy**

Civic engagement is more than just voting every few years; it encompasses a wide range of activities that allow individuals to actively participate in the political and social processes that shape their communities. From grassroots activism to public service, from community organizing to simply staying informed, civic engagement is the lifeblood of democracy.

At its core, democracy is about the collective will of the people. And voting remains the most direct and powerful expression of that will. Yet, despite the significance of voting, many citizens either do not vote or feel disengaged from the process. Voter apathy, disenfranchisement, and disillusionment with politics are all major threats to democracy.

The act of voting is more than just choosing leaders; it is a reaffirmation of one's role in shaping the direction of the country. When citizens cast their ballots, they are not only exercising a right but fulfilling a responsibility to participate in the democratic process. Voting is a direct way for individuals to hold leaders accountable, influence policy, and ensure that their voices are heard in the corridors of power.

However, voting alone is not enough. Civic engagement must be sustained between election cycles. Citizens must remain vigilant, continue to hold their leaders accountable, and advocate for policies that promote justice, equality, and the public good. Democracy is a constant dialogue, and that dialogue requires continuous engagement from its citizens.

- **Voices for Change**

Throughout history, meaningful social and political change has often been driven by grassroots movements and citizen activism. The abolition of slavery, the civil rights movement, women's suffrage, and labor rights were all the result of ordinary people coming together to challenge injustice and demand change. These movements were born out of a belief that citizens have both the right and the responsibility to challenge authority when it violates the principles of justice and equality.

Activism is not only a tool for addressing immediate concerns; it is also a way of shaping the future. Through protest, advocacy, and organizing, citizens can push for reforms that address systemic inequalities and promote a more inclusive and just society. Civic engagement through activism ensures that power remains accountable to the people and that democracy remains a living, breathing force for good.

Yet, activism also requires discipline and purpose. In an age of polarization, it is easy for activism to devolve into a zero-sum game of opposing camps shouting at one another. True civic engagement seeks dialogue, understanding, and constructive solutions, even amid deep disagreement. The most effective advocacy is built not on division but on the common goal of improving society for all.

- **Public Service: Contributing to the Common Good**

Public service is another crucial component of civic engagement. Whether through elected office, volunteer work, or community leadership, public service allows citizens to directly contribute to the well-being of their communities. It is through public service that individuals can help shape public policy, address local issues, and improve the lives of their fellow citizens.

Public service requires a commitment to the common good, putting the needs of the community above personal gain. It embodies the democratic principle that citizenship is not just about individual rights but also about collective responsibilities. When citizens engage in public service, they strengthen the fabric of society by contributing to the health, safety, and prosperity of their communities.

However, public service is not limited to those in positions of authority. Every citizen can serve in ways that benefit others. Whether through mentoring, volunteering at local organizations, or participating in community discussions, each person has a role to play in building a stronger and more resilient society. Public service is an expression of the belief that democracy is a shared responsibility, and it is through collective action that we can achieve lasting progress.

- **Building a Civically Literate Society**

Democracy cannot thrive without an informed and educated populace. Civic education is the cornerstone of a healthy democracy, providing citizens with the knowledge and skills they need to engage meaningfully in the democratic process. Yet, in many parts of the world, civic education has been neglected, leaving citizens ill-prepared to navigate the complexities of political life. To ensure the long-term health of democracy, we must prioritize education and awareness, equipping citizens with the tools they need to fulfill their civic responsibilities.

Civic education should not end when individuals leave school. Lifelong civic learning is essential for maintaining an informed and engaged citizenry. Community forums, public debates, and adult education programs can provide opportunities for citizens to continue learning about political issues, democratic principles, and their role in society.

Libraries, community centers, and civic organizations can play a key role in promoting lifelong learning. These institutions can offer workshops, discussions, and resources that help citizens stay informed about current events, government policies, and social issues. By fostering a culture of lifelong learning, we can ensure that citizens remain engaged and informed throughout their lives, contributing to the long-term health of democracy.

- **The Power and Responsibility of Citizenship**

Democracy is not a spectator sport. It requires the active participation of its citizens at every level, from voting in elections to engaging in public service, from grassroots activism to simply staying informed. The responsibility of citizenship is not only to enjoy the freedoms and rights that democracy provides but to protect and nurture those freedoms for future generations.

Civic engagement, education, and awareness are the pillars upon which a strong and resilient democracy is built. When citizens are informed, engaged, and committed to the common good, democracy flourishes. But when citizens become disengaged, apathetic, or uninformed, democracy falters. It is the responsibility of every citizen to ensure that democracy not only survives but thrives.

As we face the challenges of the modern world—rising authoritarianism, political polarization, and the erosion of public trust—it is more important than ever that we recognize the power and responsibility of citizenship. Democracy is a shared endeavor, and its future depends on our collective action. It is up to all of us to protect, preserve, and strengthen the democratic principles that have guided us for generations. The responsibility of citizenship is not just a duty; it is a privilege—one that we must uphold if we are to ensure a bright and democratic future for all.

Conclusion: The Urgency of Now: A Call to Action

History often has moments where the future hinges on the actions of the present. Moments that demand not mere observation but participation, not passive hope but active resolve. In the context of democracy, such moments are critical. They define whether a system of government painstakingly built on the principles of freedom, justice, and equality will be sustained or eroded. Today, we find ourselves at one of these crucial junctures in the coming election—an era that challenges the resilience of democracy in ways that previous generations might not have foreseen.

The urgency of now cannot be overstated. Complacency, cynicism, and inaction are not only detrimental—they are complicit in the slow erosion of democratic values. If democracy is to endure, it demands not just passive support but active citizenship.

- **The Necessity of Immediate and Sustained Action to Protect Democracy**

Active citizenship is not a slogan; it is the lifeblood of any democracy. As we have explored throughout this book, democracy relies on the engagement of its people. It thrives when citizens take ownership of their role in the political process, when they recognize that they are not simply subjects of governance but the architects of it.

- **The Time for Action Is Now**

We cannot afford to wait for others to step up. Too often, individuals assume that the responsibility to safeguard democracy falls on someone else—politicians, activists, or civic leaders. This belief is not only misguided but dangerous. Democracy's strength lies in its collective nature, in the power of many voices coming together to defend what is right. Every citizen, regardless of their position in society, has a role to play in this defense.

The threats to democracy—whether they come from within a nation's own political system, foreign interference, or the slow creep of authoritarianism—are real and imminent. Delaying action only allows these threats to grow more formidable. The fabric of democracy is delicate, and when it begins to unravel, the repair is far more difficult than the defense. ***The message is simple: we must act now.***

Active citizenship means recognizing the pressing need for action. Whether it's voting, engaging in civic dialogue, participating in community organizations, or holding elected officials accountable, every form of engagement matters. These actions may seem small in isolation, but collectively, they form the foundation upon which democracy stands.

- **Sustained Commitment: It Is a Going Concern**

The urgency of now is not just about immediate action—it's about sustained commitment. Democracy is not a battle that is fought once and won; it is an ongoing process that requires vigilance, dedication, and persistence. Many have fallen into the trap of thinking that once elections are over or once certain reforms are passed, the job of protecting democracy is complete. But the truth is that democracy is a continuous endeavor. It requires constant nurturing and care.

This sustained commitment means staying engaged even when the issues at hand seem distant or when the political landscape feels discouraging. It means educating oneself, listening to opposing viewpoints, and remaining open to dialogue. It means recognizing that democracy is not a static entity—it evolves and adapts based on the participation of its citizens.

We must resist the temptation to grow weary or complacent. There will be moments of frustration, times when progress seems slow, or when setbacks occur. But it is precisely during these moments that sustained action becomes most crucial. ***Democracy is not measured by moments of triumph alone but by the resilience shown in the face of adversity.***

- **A Final Rallying Cry**

If this book has emphasized one thing above all, it is the idea that democracy is both fragile and resilient. Fragile in that it can be undermined by neglect, but resilient in that it has the power to endure when people commit themselves to its defense. In this final section, we turn to the themes of hope and responsibility, two intertwined concepts that must guide our actions moving forward.

- **Hope**

Hope is often seen as a passive sentiment, something that resides in the realm of wishful thinking. But true hope is active—it compels us to act, to strive for a better future. It is hope that fuels movements for justice and that inspires individuals to fight against seemingly insurmountable odds. Hope, in the context of democracy, is the belief that despite the challenges we face, a better and more just society is possible.

In today's world, it is easy to be overwhelmed by the weight of political polarization, misinformation, and rising authoritarianism. But giving in to despair only ensures that these forces will prevail. Hope is not about ignoring the difficulties; it is about confronting them with the belief that change is possible. We must hold onto hope as we take on the responsibility of defending democracy. Hope reminds us that while the challenges may be great, they are not insurmountable. It gives us the strength to persist, to keep fighting for the principles that define democratic governance: freedom, equality, and justice.

The defense of democracy is not just a task for the present—it is a responsibility to future generations also. The choices we make today will determine the world they inherit. Will we pass on a democracy that is vibrant, inclusive, and just, or will we leave them with a system eroded by neglect and authoritarianism? **The responsibility is ours to bear.**

This sense of responsibility should guide our actions. It should remind us that we are not acting solely for ourselves but for those who will come after us. It is a humbling realization, but also an empowering one. We have the power to shape the future and ensure that democracy remains a system that empowers individuals and upholds the rights of all people.

This responsibility requires us to think long-term. We must not be content with quick fixes or temporary solutions. Our goal is to build a democracy that can withstand the tests of time—a system that is resilient, adaptable, and truly representative of the people it serves.

- **A Call to You: Take Up the Mantle**

As this book ends, the final call to action is directed at you, the reader. You have the power to make a difference. You are not just a spectator in the story of democracy—you are a protagonist. The decisions you make and the actions you take will shape the future of the democratic world.

The responsibility is great, but so is the potential for positive change. Each of us has a role to play, whether through voting, activism, community engagement, or simply educating ourselves and others. Democracy is a shared project, one that requires the contributions of all its citizens. Your voice and your actions matter.

This is your moment. The urgency of now demands that you rise to the occasion, that you take up the mantle of democratic defense, especially in the coming election. You may feel that your individual efforts are small, but remember that democracy is built on the collective actions of many. Together, we can protect and strengthen the institutions that have upheld freedom for generations. ***Will you answer this call?***

Democracy's future is not guaranteed, but it is within our power to secure it. The urgency of now requires that we act—immediately, purposefully, and with a deep commitment to the values that underpin democracy. We must be active citizens, fully engaged in the process of governance. We must remain hopeful, even in the face of adversity, and remember that the responsibility to protect our democracy rests with each of us.

This is not the work of a single generation, but a continuous endeavor that will require the dedication of all who believe in the power of democratic governance. The challenges we face are significant, but they are not beyond our ability to overcome. Now is the time to act. Now is the time to defend democracy for ourselves and for future generations.

The responsibility is ours, and the time is now. Let us answer the call.

About the Author

Chris S. Moses is a renowned international expert, author and advocate for democracy, social justice, and human rights. With a distinguished background in preventing child custody interference, international child abduction and domestic violence, Chris has dedicated his career to protecting vulnerable populations.

As CEO/Founder of PIPC Consulting LLC, Chris brings extensive experience in epidemiology, project management and community emergency response. His research expertise spans services for older adults, people with disabilities and their families, with a focus on mental health, geriatric diseases, and diversity/inclusion.

A seasoned trainer and peer reviewer, Chris has worked with the US Justice Department, Administration for Community Living and Office of Postsecondary Education. His anti-corruption/bribery organization leadership and advocacy for social justice in Benin Republic demonstrate his unwavering commitment to democracy.

In addition to his professional accomplishments, Chris cherishes his family life. He is a devoted husband to his loving wife and proud father of two beautiful children. His family's love and support fuel his passion for creating a better world.

Author of "Safeguarding Democracy: A Warning to America and the World" in his latest book, Chris S. Moses offers a compelling analysis of democracy's challenges and opportunities America is facing with a profound impact on the rest of the world. Drawing from his vast expertise, Chris provides actionable strategies for preserving democracy and promoting social justice.